THE MANAGEMENT OF
PROBLEM-SOLVING

THE MANAGEMENT
OF
PROBLEM-SOLVING

POSITIVE RESULTS
FROM PRODUCTIVE THINKING

GRAHAM TARR

A HALSTED PRESS BOOK

JOHN WILEY & SONS
New York – Toronto

First published 1973 by
The Macmillan Press Ltd

Published in the U.S.A. and
Canada by Halsted Press, a
Division of John Wiley & Sons, Inc.,
New York

Printed in Great Britain

Library of Congress Cataloging in Publication Data

Tarr, Graham.
  The management of problem-solving.

  'A Halsted Press book.'
  1. Management. 2. Problem solving. I. Title.
HD38.T26 1973   658.4'03   73–2956
ISBN 0–470–84555–4

Contents

Foreword   vii

Author's Preface   ix

Dramatis Personae   xi

1 The Think-Tank Approach   1

2 Profile of a Problem-Solving Group   15

3 Human Relationships   32

4 Effective Control   54

5 Creative Thinking   84

6 Dangerous Thinking   108

7 The End Result   136

References   152

Subject Index   157

Foreword

This book draws on the author's experience over a number of years in working with and controlling problem-solving groups on a wide variety of subjects. A good deal of this experience was gained in his work with this company.

The opinions expressed are his own, but many of them reflect a realistic and practical approach which I would like to think bears the EASAMS hallmark. Others are controversial, even a little provocative, and of course we do not necessarily agree with everything he has written. But controversy in this field is no bad thing, and by provoking the reader from time to time Graham Tarr has at least prevented any accusation of dullness.

On this score, and because there is so much good sense to be found in it, we welcome the publication of this book as a valuable contribution to the problem of thinking straight about thinking straight.

D. J. CASHMORE
Director
EASAMS Ltd

Camberley, Surrey
October 1972

Author's Preface

The mathematical and logical techniques of solving problems have been very fully documented, but it seems that little has been written on the task of getting the work done, and done well, whatever the techniques used. This is a management problem, and I believe that the proper aim of such a manager is to make the work of problem-solving more *effective* – in the quality of thought, in the use of human resources, and in the final outcome of getting the solution adopted.

To advise this manager I have produced a book which is intended to be wise rather than learned. My qualification for wisdom does not proceed from any special virtue, but from the chance variety of my experience. The transitions I have had to make from engineering, to applied technological research, to a techno-military 'think-tank', and thence to civil operational research and economics, have certainly helped. The more recent opportunity to work at several different levels in quick succession, having switched from heading a group of projects in the United Kingdom to leading a United Nations team and back again, has given further insight, while at the same time the change from consultant to customer and back has helped me to appreciate both sides of several arguments.

I hope that people in other fields, particularly in line management, will dip into this book enough to gain some understanding of the special problems arising from the nature of problem-solving work, the central characteristic of which is the fact that every day breaks new ground and that little progress can be made without deep intellectual harmony between two or more members of a team.

If any of my former colleagues should read this book, they should not try to identify themselves or their work with any of the classes of people and situations mentioned. The pictures I have painted are synthesised from elements of experience in many different projects and several organisations.

G.T.

Geneva
1972

Dramatis Personae

In the interplay between personalities engaged in organised problem-solving, several different names are used to describe people filling essentially the same role. Since a clear label for each of the main actors in the piece will be helpful, I have adopted the following terms throughout:

THE DECISION-MAKER. He is the one who has a problem to be solved. He can be considered as the customer of the problem-solving group. The name often given to the same character is 'the manager'. I prefer to avoid this, since it tends to mask the fact that management should be taking place everywhere, not least inside the problem-solving group itself.

THE GROUP LEADER. The work of solving the decision-maker's problems may be carried out in an independent consultancy group working for a variety of customers, in a 'think-tank' organisation usually set up to work on behalf of one or two major sponsors, or in a parent organisation where the unit is given a variety of names: 'the operational research department', 'the systems group', 'the management services team' and 'the long-range planning unit', for example. The term 'group', which I use throughout, is intended to cover any of these, and the head of the group I propose to call the 'group leader'.

THE PROJECT LEADER. Within the group there will usually be several distinct tasks, studies or problems being worked on at any one time. I use the term 'project' for any of these, and call the individual with technical responsibility for the project the 'project leader'. In the case of a unit assembled for the purpose of carrying out a single project, with no intention of permanence, then the project leader may become his own group leader.

THE ANALYST. The professional staff who carry out the work of the problem-solving group are often hard put to know what to call themselves. However, whatever else they do, they have to analyse situations and problems before reaching conclusions, and therefore I propose to use the term 'analyst' throughout. There is no intention that this implies 'systems analyst', which is most often applied to those who specifically apply computer techniques.

THE ADMINISTRATOR. Also making an occasional brief appearance is the character who has the responsibility for providing the group with its daily needs, but has no responsibility for its technical work. I call him the 'administrator'.

1 The Think-Tank Approach

'Yes, but we have got to think of the effect on the ordinary nice people we meet in the street. They are not terribly brainy, but they are quite nice people really.'
Stephen Potter, *One-Upmanship*

The problems given to the group to solve can be as narrow as finding the mathematically optimum level at which to reorder an item of stock in a spare-parts store, and as wide as a comparison of the varying social goals of a national health service. Problems of the first type can usually be satisfactorily solved by the application of quantitative operational research techniques, while those of the second are more likely to need the services of a so-called 'think-tank' – a group with a reputation for creativity and breadth of thinking.

In between these two extremes lies the range of partly quantitative, partly qualitative, imprecisely defined problems which operational research men may try to solve with a model and the man trained rather in the humanities may try to reason out in words. In truth, neither approach is highly successful in isolation, and one of my main aims is to describe how to achieve a blend of the two which will lead to an improvement in the quality of the solutions. The resultant approach will be found to have shifted rather closer to that of the think-tank.

Judging by the weaknesses of the past work, the areas where improvement is most needed are those of creativity, social awareness, the need for realism, and the speed and economy with which the work is done.

The need for creativity is frequently left out of the specification of a task, and indeed if the team inject a fresh idea they may find that the decision-maker is put out. He may have good cause, but more likely the reason is that he only feels comfortable with those solutions to his problems which are traditional and have been shown to work in the past. This attitude leads to requests for the analyst to evaluate the outcome of given alternative solutions without questioning the grounds on which these alternatives have been chosen. There are cases where this approach is perfectly reasonable, of course: for example, where the group is brought in at a late stage – when, say, it is no longer a question of whether to go for a centralised stockholding facility, but to compare in quantitative terms whether to site it in London, Leicester or Birmingham. (Even in this situation there is scope for some original thinking, but the point is made.)

In other cases, even though it is quite early enough for a fresh idea to be considered, the decision-maker may circumscribe the problem too closely and put forward only his own alternative solutions to be evaluated. When this happens there is a strong argument for the group leader to seek permission to search for further solutions. He will probably be given only a reluctant go-ahead, and he must be wary of letting his analysts appear to be wasting effort on the novelties. But he will have opened the door to an unknown world which on rare occasions contains a really valuable idea. The attempt is always worth while.

Such freedom to innovate in overall solutions is the

more dramatic form of creativity, but equally important is the persistent creativity needed at every stage
of the work if the problem-solving is to be truly effective. This is a subject deserving treatment in its own
right, and Chapter 5 is devoted to it.

Until an alternative solution is evaluated, no one
can be too sure that it was a good one to have been
tabled, and until a solution has been tabled it cannot
be evaluated – a vicious circle, which has to be broken
by a succession of compromises and approximations.
But the analyst should appreciate that this give-and-
take process in itself adds strength to the final answer.
The main task of finding the best solution to a problem is often one of gradually filtering out the less
attractive so as to narrow the list of options, but if a
good dialogue is maintained between the decision-
maker and the analyst, a learning process can go on
during the filtering which generally leads to an improved statement of the requirement itself.

This learning process can be illustrated in a funnel-
shaped diagram (Fig. 1) which I have used more
specifically in technological fields, but which can be
interpreted more generally.

The lower curve in the diagram expresses the
point that the problem to be solved can rarely be
defined precisely at the start of the project: not
merely because of the vicious circle, but because
solutions take time to institute and their useful life
will be in the uncertain environment of the future.
So it is generally wrong for the decision-maker to say:
'This is my requirement – 100 per cent specified.
Now meet it.' And it is equally wrong for the analyst
to ask for such a clear-cut specification too early. If a
dialogue between the decision-maker and the analyst
starts early enough, then the requirement will move

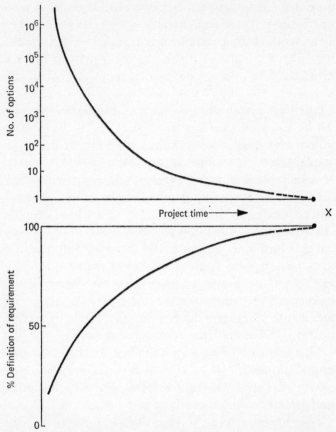

FIG. 1. THE OVERALL PROBLEM: to eliminate all the options but one, and at the same time achieve a 100 per cent definition of the requirement.

from roughly defined at the start – the broad intention only – to approach 100 per cent (but never reach it: there will always be room for manœuvre) as project time progresses.

The upper curve shows that, in a project where the dialogue is taking place, the project starts with a host of alternative solutions to the roughly defined requirement, and that as the work proceeds and alternatives are evaluated (roughly at first, then increasingly accurately), the less promising can be eliminated. But this evaluation, particularly at the early rough stage, can contribute strongly to the decision-maker's understanding of his environment, and even more to his understanding of the type and scope of the solutions which are possible. He will then be able to shift his ground slightly, raise or lower his sights, adjust his priorities, and define his requirement more closely. For example, in the planning of new seaport facilities the work of evaluating alternative proposals forces the traffic demand to be more closely specified, and this may show that the existing port with some operational changes can handle the traffic.

A project which proceeds smoothly along these funnel-shaped curves, rather than switching jerkily from one to the other, or remaining stuck at one point, is more likely to get closer to the unattainable goal of point X, where there is one 'correct' solution to a 100 per cent defined problem. That is to say, in the magnificent opening lines of a historic proposal: 'Planning is an iterative process of multiple phase.'

All too often we may meet the decision-maker who says: 'Now you know the problem; go away and solve it', and would prefer to know no more until a written report lands on his desk. Incredibly, I once heard these words applied to a complex economic study planned to last over twelve months. On that occasion it was possible to persuade the decision-maker of the greater value of the dialogue, and in the event the first of the regular meetings which were set up disclosed that the problem as stated was wildly off the mark. The requirement was in fact to compete for a shrinking market, not as originally stated to invest in the face of an expanding one. This was perhaps an extreme.

Another major weakness of much of the work done is the failure to include in the description of a system under study the untidy behaviour and the complex motives of humans. Without this, the solution is likely to reflect a precise academic view of the situation which is far from the truth; and when implemented it may produce effects widely differing from those predicted. Luckily for the humans involved, decision-makers more often than not appreciate the social problems of such solutions and will not implement them.

The cry then goes up from the analyst: 'They never implement my proposals.' But the analyst should ask himself why the decision-maker commissioned him to work out a solution but was not prepared for the particular answer given. The fault will usually be found to lie in the analyst. **A solution which is not implemented is a poor solution,** since the factors affecting implementation could have been made an integral part of the problem and solved alongside it. It is usually the analyst who has chosen (or has meekly agreed) to deal with the problems of implementation as an add-on task after the analysis is finished and the conclusions drawn. (As with all dogma, an exception exists – when the decision-maker is dethroned before the solution can be introduced. But let us not torture ourselves with this.)

Failure to pay enough attention to the social aspects of a problem also lowers the general quality of the answer – the 'rightness' of a solution. An example of this is in the introduction of modern passenger-handling methods at a seaport catering for tourist cruise ships. However efficient this is as seen by the Customs, and however good an economic case can be made, this destroys much of the charm of the jostling rowing-boats which traditionally ferry passengers to and from the quay. Who can doubt that if the customer were consulted the last thing he would have voted for is the atmosphere of an international airport during his holiday cruises?

A purist may reply to this point that the romantic factor was not among the criteria of success which it was agreed he should apply in assessing the alternatives. But who has agreed the criteria? Very probably they were hammered out at an early meeting between the group leader and the decision-maker. Even if the group leader might not be expected to have thought of such a criterion then, he should at least have secured agreement that additional criteria could be added later.

There will often be genuine differences of opinion over criteria, but there is always one ultimate criterion of 'rightness': whether all the people involved (decision-maker, operatives and customers) like the proposal and will accept it. The analyst often has much more freedom in working to this criterion than is admitted. The trouble is, of course, that the goals of some of the individuals involved will conflict with wider social goals and there has to be a compromise. Placing the emphasis on the large-scale social view of a problem is at once the easier course and the one most likely to be carried too far, with a tendency even to allow abstract principles to override concrete facts ('a peculiarly Russian trait', according to Bochenski). This is not to say that we should always go to Bochenski's exact opposite of 'the empirical English who, not using theory as their starting-point, seek to solve all problems on the basis of concrete reality and of experience gained in their immediate surroundings'.

The need for many analysts to move nearer to the English empirical approach is clearly demonstrated by a scene where it is often clear to all but the research team that the decision will be made on grounds other than their numerical evaluation; when a textbook devoted to the social aspect of industry can ignore the existence of illegal incentive payments; and when a major company can make the comment on its new product: 'It came out very well in the market survey, but somehow the actual customers didn't seem to like it.' Surely the time has come for researchers of all kinds to take off their blinkers and extend the analytical boundaries of their problems to include the world of real people with human motives.

A solution which takes account of human behaviour gets closer to reality by doing so. But there is another aspect of reality in which bad work by the analyst is even more deadly because the decision-maker cannot put his finger on it. This is the accuracy – or lack of it – with which the quantitative and mechanistic description of the problem reflects its real nature. Here the analyst purports to be the expert who cannot be questioned on the quality of his work, but rather asks for an act of confidence by the decision-maker. By doing so he shoulders a heavy responsibility. He had better be right, for decisions will (or should) be made on the basis of the answers he gets.

But every description of reality is a compromise and a simplification. I shall return to this subject again in Chapter 6; the point I want to make here is that the analyst has to find a way of being scrupulously honest with the decision-maker over the reliance which the latter can place in the results. And this has to be done without destroying the decision-maker's confidence in the analysis as a whole. This requires not only fine judgement, but a degree of understanding on both sides which is not likely to develop unless the decision-maker has been involved progressively at each stage of the study. Much of the reason for a less than perfect system description arises from the assumptions which had to be made to pave the way for a manageable analysis. It is in any case dangerous to make assumptions without discussing them with people who know the environment well, but even if the analyst can make sensible assumptions throughout, it is expecting a great deal of the decision-maker to have to assimilate a long list of assumptions and caveats if he only hears them for the first time when the conclusions are presented to him. If on the other hand he has been involved in making the assumptions, and the main compromises have been explained to him along the way, the decision-maker will have a good idea of what sort of reliance he should place in the conclusions and what degree of risk he will be taking if he acts on them.

Involving the decision-maker in the work has a further obvious advantage, but one which can easily be overlooked by an analyst engrossed in his own methods. This is that the line manager, being normally an expert in his subject, can himself make a valuable contribution. Although he has called in the problem-solving group to do the analysis, he is likely to have a deep understanding of the system, its environment and the factors which determine the plausibility of solutions – particularly, of course, the qualitative factors. Nothing is more irritating to the decision-maker than the analyst who believes he knows quite enough about the subject and needs no help from the man who spends his life thinking about it. Almost invariably this is not true.

On his side the decision-maker should be led to understand the strengths of the analyst. He will easily accept the greater precision of the quantitative and mechanistic approach, and the ability of the analyst to handle a broader and more complex set of relationships than can be held in the head. But he may not find it so easy when in the course of the work the analyst displays another of his qualities – the imagination and persistence to question traditional beliefs. For it is essential that the analyst searches for the factors which in the past led to a particular way of thinking or doing things. This will lead him to answer 'Why?' to the statement: 'This is the way we do it here.' He will find that the answer to the question 'Why?' is often prejudiced, occasionally mistaken. This questioning and the fresh thinking which it leads to will be uncomfortable for the decision-maker, and care may be needed to point out why the analyst is doing it.

The level of sophistication of the decision-maker and his organisation, together with its flexibility, must be taken into account by the analyst when proposing a solution. In rare cases an organisation may have decided that, come what may, it will wrench itself into the latest methods throughout all departments. In this case it has assessed the risk and the analyst can feel free. But normally the responsibility rests with the analyst, who has an overview of the organisation's level of sophistication and the relation it bears to the degrees of modernisation available. There is danger in trying to pull any one part or function of an organisation a long way ahead of the remainder, since this can produce strain. The modernisation of the part so treated is likely to be eroded by the links it has with the remainder, and the result may be the failure of the systems introduced.

This is a well-known phenomenon on work for developing countries, where the great weight of the existing level of culture acts as a drag on the too rapid advancement of any single assistance project. The effect can be thought of as a large flat sheet of elastic, which when lifted up at one point will stay raised as long as the external force is applied, but will sink back to the common level when the force is removed.

The forces resisting change are often stronger than the analyst imagines, both in the tendency of a system to resist attempts to improve it, and in the resilience of a system to setbacks. This was illustrated after the British coal-miners' strike of 1972 when the degree of temporary dislocation was severe but the industrial system returned to normal much faster than expected. A control systems engineer would explain this by saying that the industrial system has a transfer function (response to stimuli) which responds in a similar way to a positive stimulus as to a negative one. This leads to the conclusion that, since it is extremely difficult to step up the nation's production without a prolonged positive stimulus, it is also difficult to depress it by a short negative one.

When faced with the problem of partial modernisation, the analyst should try to find a solution which is a reasonable distance ahead of the current practices but is within the management's ability to assimilate. If he can suggest successive stages of modernisation which lead on by manageable steps, so much the better. But he should make an attempt to communicate to the decision-maker the danger of going too far too fast.

A solution which is not implemented is a poor solution. Apart from the social reasons for failure to implement, there is the more obvious reason. This is that the solution posed fell outside the limits of the decision-maker's freedom of manœuvre. The fact that there is a jargon expression – 'the user's policy-space' – for this limitation shows that, in operational research at least, the problem has been well recognised.

The more usual form of this is that a decision-maker has genuine authority to make the necessary change (or can easily obtain it), but has financial and political contraints which prevent him accepting a solution which goes too far. All that need be said here is that the analyst who takes pains to open a sound dialogue with the decision-maker will surely find a way of quizzing him on what is feasible and what is not.

A less usual but by no means rare form is that of the decision-maker who has the authority to ask for a solution to a problem but not the authority to make any change suggested. The group leader should be very much on his guard against this. If his team know it, all is well because the problems of getting the solution carried through – whether they are political, financial or organisational – can be brought into the sphere of discussion and will have an appropriate impact on the study from the start. But if the realisation that the man who commissioned the study is not the decision-maker emerges late, it can seriously damage both the inherent sense of the conclusions and the morale of the team. The simple way of finding out whether the authority exists is to ask at the setting-up stage of the project for an explanation of the decision procedure which will be followed when the conclusions are presented. This is a reasonable request at this stage, and when answered should set things in perspective.

The fourth main area in which I have suggested that improvement is most needed is the speed and economy with which the group's work is done.

Little thought appears to have been given to the plain and simple management of such groups. The group leader is not likely to fall into the trap of a rigid and hierarchical management style – McGregor's 'Theory X' as opposed to the more liberal and collegiate 'Theory Y' – but there is still a good deal of scope for him to consider what are the special characteristics of his group, what special management style is most productive of fast, high-quality work, and what methods of planning, control and organisation are most likely to be successful. These subjects are discussed in the following chapters.

Not least among the factors affecting the productivity of a problem-solving group are the working tools it is given and the environment it has to work in. This subject is a little outside my main theme in this book, but the group leader should not dismiss the problem so lightly. He will find that some objectivity tinged with consideration can pay big dividends both in quality and quantity of output.

To close this chapter, in which I have reviewed the main ways in which a problem-solving group can try to improve the quality of its solutions and give them more breadth, let me make a final and more searching point. Those whose solutions to a requirement are implemented are to that extent changing the world. Thus they have a responsibility to consider the nature of the future world they are helping to create.

There is no need to swell any further the flood of literature on the environment, but only to pick on the one danger which seems to me to deserve greater emphasis. This is the possibility that we may end up with too much system. A comment by Fruchtbaum puts the point well: 'Technology may so change the nature of man and society that the very concept of choice and action will be totally altered and the possibility of open-ended options precluded.'

This takes us back full circle to the fears Chaplin expressed many years ago in the unforgettable automatic eating sequence in his film *Modern Times*. But the fear is still with us, and the analyst who proposes a way of doing things which he knows in his heart will deprive human life of some of its richness, without looking for the alternative or at the very least pointing out the problem, is doing the world a disservice. The 'possibility of open-ended options' is a fundamental criterion of goodness which could well be applied to the solution of any human problem.

Put another way, as a wise man said about the legal system: 'Our liberties reside in the interstices of procedure.'

2 Profile of a Problem-Solving Group

Examine their counsels and their cares; digest things
    rightly
Touching the weal of the common; you shall find
No public benefit which you receive
But it proceeds or comes from them to you,
And no way from yourselves.

Coriolanus, Act i, scene i

In this chapter I shall try to paint a picture of the corporate nature of a problem-solving group and show how its standards of performance are affected by the way it is organised.

It is seldom satisfactory for a single analyst to work in isolation. Two or three analysts working on a problem usually seem to have a strong catalytic effect on each other so that the whole is greater than the sum of the parts. Often this takes the form of one simply acting as a foil to the ideas of another, but equally often the two or three members of such a cell can complement each other by supplying different viewpoints which – because their owners know that they have eventually to agree – have to be hammered out in discussions until a single truth is forged. This reconciliation calls for a willingness to re-examine assumptions and first principles and takes the members of the cell more deeply into the subject.

This interplay is of course not new – it happens every day in academic circles – but in the problem-solving cell it tends to be more goal-oriented and because of this can be much more powerful. Further, since the protagonists are members of a single team with a vested interest in finding a single agreed conclusion (and not in maintaining a line of reasoning for long enough to establish their personal academic stamp), the result is much more likely to be successful.

More than three analysts working in depth on one aspect of a problem is usually counter-productive since the degree of flexibility and intellectual harmony which can be maintained falls off rapidly with the size of the cell. We are then left with a picture of a project team which varies from a single cell of two or three analysts probing together all aspects of the problem, to a large team made up of several cells each probing a particular aspect, but all linked into a co-ordinated team.

This linking will be twofold. Firstly, from the natural law that every part of a problem is related to every other part, so that as well as having their responsibility for in-depth analysis of their own aspect, each cell will find itself drawn into a study at lesser depth of the problems and conclusions of one or two neighbouring cells. And secondly, a link between all cells is provided by the project leader, who must have a sound understanding of the thinking of each.

This is a big demand on the project leader of a team of more than, say, ten analysts, and in fact project teams rarely get larger than this. Attempts have been made to set up large teams by turning the project leader rather into a 'project co-ordinator' to concentrate on project control, while allowing each cell within the team to remain intellectually independent. The necessary meeting of minds is then achieved by relying on the natural links between problem cells, topped up by full round-table discussions (and a strong editor of the final report). In my experience this does not lead to the best quality of work, both because of the lack of the overview of the intellectually involved project leader, and also because it seems to leave individual cells floating free, with shifting boundaries around their special problem area.

The need for this cellular approach, where in every aspect of the problem at least two views have to be reconciled, is partly dependent on the level of experience and skill of the individuals. When a member of the group is outstanding at his specialty, then he can of course be left to work alone, taking sole responsibility for all the thinking on that aspect. But there are dangers in this. The full reasoning behind his conclusions (which can rarely be spelt out adequately in writing) may be hidden for ever in his brain – an obvious risk. But more serious than this is the loss of the corporate strength of the team. A man working intellectually alone is no more than an individual consultant, and it is not unknown for a team to be formed wholly of such individuals. Such 'teams' of individuals are to be found out in the field giving confident solutions to problems, but in fact they may not be teams at all. It is not unknown for reports to be issued which are made up of a series of totally independent sections on different aspects of the problem, the only co-ordination being that of the perplexed editor. As an extreme, I know of one 'team leader' who had to put to bed a project report in which one section had been written by a team member he had never met (the latter had finished his part of the work and gone before the rest were recruited). In general, unless there is a brilliant project leader who can sense mismatch between the assumptions and conclusions of the individual experts and correct it early enough, such an approach is likely to be much weaker than when specialists whose areas overlap each examine in depth the reasoning of the other, thus forming again (for that period) an intellectual cell.

We now have a broad picture of a project team, and can consider the group as a whole, composed of several such teams.

Just as the project leader finds it difficult to span too many cells, so the group leader finds it difficult to span too many projects. This differs from the traditional management problem of the span of authority only in that there is the additional element of *intellectual span*, not merely the span of responsibility and general control. Since it is impossible for the group leader to be familiar in depth with the reasoning of each cell of each project team, he either has to find a way of keeping to broad conclusions and main lines of thought – to find a way of going so far and no further into each project – or he has to find a criterion for filtering out those elements in each project which he will try to understand and contribute to in depth, and those that he will leave strictly alone.

But first a more fundamental question may be raised. Should the group leader – a manager two removes from the point of action – try in any sense to contribute intellectually to that action? I am sure that he should. The group leader's participation (and indeed that of anyone higher up the organisation who has the appropriate skills) can count for a great deal; in the majority of cases when the group leader takes a special interest in the detail of a problem he can make a very valuable contribution. It is surprising – and sometimes irritating to the junior – the extent to which the widely experienced senior can lift the standard of a week's work in a single hour's session. I shall be referring to this in Chapter 4 as a basic ingredient of project control.

Having decided that his role does include contributing in depth, it follows that the group leader must adopt the second of the two approaches and probe deeply into some aspects but not others. How to make this selection need not be too agonising a choice. If he has sensitive enough feelers he can tell which activities are most in need of strengthening and which are not. He will also be guided by the knowledge of his own skills and where they are most likely to be applied profitably. And since he is in regular discussion with his project leaders at a more general level, he can make specific offers of help and receive guidance from the project leader on which activity to select.

When he does decide to contribute to the project, the busy group leader should be aware of a special danger. By virtue of being so busy he may be led to postpone important working discussions, pleading unavoidable engagements. This happens so often in some cases that projects have been slowed to a snail's pace while an analyst waits frustratedly for the next audience. Such paths are paved with good intentions, but this is not enough. The group leader should never make a promise to, say, 'devote 10 per cent of my time to it' unless he is quite sure that he is going to fulfil this commitment. If he falls down on this, the group leader can do more harm than good in trying to play a direct part.

Much of the group leader's involvement will be direct between him and a cell which may not include the project leader. This is a healthy link which should not in any way worry the project leader. It is on a par with the principle of short-circuiting rigid hierarchical levels of management. It can be highly beneficial, as described by Anthony Jay in *Management and Machiavelli*, in the chapter entitled 'The Fearful Symmetry'. The symmetry in question is that of the pyramid where the manager at each level had three subordinates reporting to him, so that in a seven-level organisation there is 'a row of 729 junior managers and an urgent need for a very large and triangular piece of paper'. In such an organisation, according to Jay, 'the sight of one of their subordinates talking to the boss sets their ulcers twitching'. The cellular structure he advocates (using 'cell' in a slightly different sense) allows communication from the peripheral cells where the action is taking place direct to a central organisation without going through intermediaries. This is very close to the needs of the problem-solving group.

A project leader who has been indoctrinated with this liberal approach will not feel that on every element of his project he has to know more than the group leader. He should rather try to find out himself in what areas the group leader can contribute most and ask him if he is prepared to help. After all, any additional strength he can put into his project, wherever it is found (provided that he is not going to be charged too much for it), must be a good thing.

For as regards technical success (that is, delivery of the right solution in the right form and on time), the project leader has full responsibility and should be fostered in the belief that it genuinely is **his** project. The project leader is preferably full-time on the one project, or if not the fraction devoted to other tasks must be clearly set at a lower priority, so that there should never be any doubt where a project leader's loyalties lie.

A group leader who has some knowledge of management science will have appreciated the 'fearful symmetry' arguments against building hierarchies in large organisations, but may not be able to get the emphasis right in his small group. In an attempt to avoid introducing a further level into the hierarchy he may refrain from nominating a project leader even when a clear-cut project has crystallised. He may feel, for example, that he himself is taking part in the work so is effectively acting as project leader. But he is bound to have several other responsibilities of at least as high a priority and is in fact only acting as a part-time consultant plus policy-maker. It is probably the senior full-time member of the team who is the effective project leader. Unless he is specifically nominated he will have no clear authority to set up programmes of work, allocate tasks, and generally bring the improvement which only a full-time project leader can bring. With a really experienced set of consultants a loose partnership on a project can work, but it is always advisable to elect a leader and hold him responsible even if his boss is contributing to the work.

More generally, specialists contributing to a project must always be considered as subject to the authority of the project leader for their work programme, irrespective of their seniority. This authority can extend to the methodology as well if the specialist is linking his work into that of the team as a whole, but of course if possible the project leader should not constrain the specialist's freedom, provided it delivers the goods on time. If the staff concerned are not experienced in this type of relationship, it should be spelt out at the start: time-scales, the degree of co-ordination required, and the extent of the project leader's responsibility for the specialist's techniques.

The extent to which the project leader should be given full responsibility for general management matters, such as budget or recruiting, depends on the local situation. The principle which usually pays the most dividend is to pass responsibilities down the line as far as possible, although there will be some reservations. Certainly, as regards the control of costs, responsibility should be passed down even as far as the senior partner of a cell within a project: the cell has a task to complete and should have a broad idea of how much money it is using up in completing it.

Although there can be a gradual progression of depth of responsibility from team member to project leader to group leader, there are two distinctly different characteristics of the group leader's job. The first is the extent to which he must split his time between several projects which often differ widely both in technique and in area of application. The second is the need to control the nature of the work which the group agrees to undertake.

When a decision has to be made in the problem-solving group it is not generally enough for the group leader to listen to a summary of the facts and then pass a judgement. He will wherever possible want to check the quality of the reasoning which has gone into such a summary, and query the accuracy of techniques used and assumptions made. And since he will not have been deeply involved in every aspect of every project, the question may be new to him. While the project leader can be likened to a whale swimming in the depths and only coming up occasionally to breathe, the group leader is more like a seagull ranging over the waters, but diving in occasionally to catch a fish.

For it *is* vital for the project leader to come up occasionally, to raise his head out of the sea of detail and view the problem from a broader angle; and it is the group leader's job to make sure that he does this. He must regularly detach his project leaders from too deep a preoccupation with their techniques and encourage them to think wisely rather than elegantly. If there is one central theme in the technical control which the group leader must exercise, it is this: 'Slow down. Think. Re-examine your approach.'

This is not to advocate constant changes of direction; indeed, there are many problems where several approaches (all more or less imperfect) can be used, and where any one of them will be successful if pursued to a conclusion. It is rather to guard against the more frequent danger that a team becomes committed to continuing in the direction in which it set off even though a less committed mind would see that it has turned out to be the wrong direction. To give an example, a team was building a computer simulation to study the expected performance of a large new control system. They found that one piece of equipment that went to make up the whole, when modelled by putting together the expected responses of its component circuits as given by the designer, kept going unstable. A difficult and advanced piece of analysis was undertaken to find out why the equipment was unstable. After a while this became almost an end in itself and an expert was working on it full-time (enjoying himself thoroughly). But there was a painfully simple change of direction needed. This was to cut out all the detail in this particular part of the system and simply model the specified design response of the whole piece of equipment; by doing this the whole system simulation could be put on the road again while the expert and the designer argued at their leisure. In fact, it was later found that all the experiments which were needed could be carried out without the extra detail and it was never put back. (In reality, of course, the equipment had never been unstable and there was an error in the descriptive data of the circuitry.)

Another example was in the modelling of the turn-round time of ships at a berth. A team had for some time known that the queueing theory currently in use did not hold in the real situation (because of several complications like the correlation between queue length and service time) and had argued themselves into a rigid position that there was no analytic solution, and the only hope lay in experiments with a full-scale simulation. When a new team member arrived and was given this particular set of experiments to concentrate on, he was able to suggest an intermediate approach which used some features of queueing theory and some experiments on a greatly simplified simulation. His intermediate method produced accurate enough answers for most purposes and at very much less time and effort. The team itself could easily have thought of this, but they were committed and so they did not.

In the first example it needed courage and modesty to drop the detail; in the second it needed a fresh approach. A team too heavily committed will find these departures impossible: they gradually grow intellectual blinkers which prevent them from seeing anywhere but straight ahead. This is the awful danger, and this is why a wise group leader insists on his project leaders frequently emerging from their detail and taking a broader view.

The second special responsibility of the group leader is to control the work which the group agrees to undertake. A group is unlikely to want to continue for ever on exactly similar work since eventually staleness and lack of fresh thinking can set in, which not only makes the work more of a drudge but also tends to develop a set of dogmas. This is dangerous; the group will start to propose set solutions for situations which call for different approaches, and in the end the mantle may have to pass to a new group. (There is also the more practical point that the group may run out of problems.) The staleness can to some extent be kept at bay if the methods and analytical techniques themselves change from time to time. It may seem merely to be pandering to human weaknesses, but a team working in a well-worn problem area can be enlivened tremendously if they are encouraged to employ new techniques. An example of this is the advent of scenario writing,[1] which gave new life to teams who had grown stale in the practice of economic forecasting. Taken too far, it can lead to gimmickry. Still, those groups who have been successful over a very long period working in the same field are also those who were up in the forefront of methodology and always willing to develop new approaches.

If the work is going to change, there is a choice for the group leader between letting it evolve freely or steering it. Two forces are at work to produce the evolution. The first is self-evident: what problems are brought to him? He may accept everything which the group has the capacity to handle (or if the group has to show a profit, all that looks profitable). Or if he has chosen to be against free evolution, then he will have to make a determined stand against accepting projects which lead in the unwanted direction. This requires real will-power, particularly as there is almost sure to be one of his analysts who would have dearly liked to tackle that particular problem.

The second force at work is the resultant of the personal preferences of individual members of the group. This is an influence which the group leader

---

[1] This consists of setting out a descriptive self-consistent story about the possible future situation, with a little imagination built in, to supplement and amplify a quantitative projection.

must consider carefully before resisting, since fighting it can damage morale. The tendency may be conscious; an analyst may be saying to himself: 'Here I am just coming to the end of a project to determine the comparative safety of air and land travel. For my next project I would like to work further on air safety since I find this particularly interesting.' Or it may be unconscious; if there are several aspects of study, the analyst may do a better job on the one that he likes, so that it is the customer who says: 'That work they did for me was damned good on the air aspects. They seem to have quite a capability there. They're just the people to have a go at that problem of collecting aircraft failure statistics.' And so the two influences feed each other.

Since personal preferences and capabilities have this effect, the group leader influences the evolution of the group every time he recruits a new member. When extra staff are needed to cope with the work, candidates tend to be considered on the basis of suitability for the existing work of the group, not their aspirations for the future (which they may not themselves have consciously thought out). But when the appointment is made, the resultant of all the individual staff tendencies is immediately shifted slightly, how far depending on the strength of personality of the recruit. This should be a point to examine during the interview, by introducing the question: 'Leaving aside the immediate project you would be working on, what sort of work would you prefer to be doing next year or the year after?'

So the effect of new recruits must be watched carefully. But beware even more of the fanatic, or the analyst with a bee in his bonnet. If given his head he can have an enormous influence and can distort the evolution of the group beyond all reason. I recall one such who had a passion for the calculus of variations. Until this came clearly to the surface it was puzzling why in several projects the technique was being discussed as a useful aid in the most unlikely places. After a while the devotee was able to say: 'Since this is the coming tool which seems to have many applications, surely we ought to have a basic capability in it. Why not let me carry out a proper assessment of the technique and work up a standard variational calculus package?' When the penny dropped, it was clear that the sole reason for the apparent general interest was this man's personal advocacy, flitting from project team to project team. That technique was no more useful now than it had ever been. The devotee was resisted – at the cost of his voluntary departure shortly afterwards for more amenable academic stamping-grounds – and the group heaved a sigh of relief and went back to solving problems with more commonplace but equally effective tools.

Unless the problems being handed to the group without being solicited are enough to sustain its preferred rate of growth, then some form of marketing will be needed. The group leader will normally be most closely concerned with this, although the project leaders have their part to play: indirectly by producing work of an excellence which generates more, and directly by discussing further possibilities with the decision-maker whom they should now know well. I will say no more on the question of selling, since I am trying to suggest ways of raising the quality of the work, not its quantity. On the contrary, I want to sound a warning. I have seen several cases where the group leader from natural ambition has been led to spend so large a part of his personal effort on chasing new work that he has not been able to make a worth-while contribution to any of his projects; and since he was the most capable and experienced analyst in the group, the quality of the work began to wear thin. He had gone too far. There is clearly a balance to be struck here, and doing so is one of the most difficult decisions the group leader has to make.

In problem-solving organisations the general doctrine that an organisation must either grow or die need not hold: there are examples of groups remaining stable for very substantial periods. But in many cases growth will be felt desirable. If a group is to grow, then we must ask how rapid a rate of growth can be sustained before the performance of the group will be weakened. I think that we must recognise here a difference between project-based and function-based organisations. The strength of the project-based organisation in this respect is its ability to grow in discrete steps by forming additional project teams, without the need to consider hierarchical levels of authority. As long as the number of projects is still within the span of control of the group leader, nothing need change. This type of growth can be thoroughly healthy, particularly since at the time of forming the new project team it is possible for the project leader to be taken from within the group by picking an analyst who has shown himself ready for the job. By lacing the new team with new recruits there is the real possibility of growth without deterioration. It can be thought of as a 'natural' or 'spontaneous' growth, since only when a new project leader is ready to be born can the new team be set up.

There are, on the other hand, ways of forcing the growth to an artificial rate, but each leads somewhat to a lowering of quality. If the expansion is forced by recruiting more juniors, then, firstly, this year's team member doing an excellent specialised analysis has to become next year's project leader before he has enough experience to handle the whole project. Secondly, this year's project leader has to become next year's group leader handling several projects without enough time for any one of them. The combined effect can be disastrous, not least in its impact on the customer. It is not unknown for a major change in staff level to take place between the start and finish of a project, with the result that the project leader, although nominally still responsible for the detailed project work, ends up snatching only a day here and there on the project, finally hurriedly editing a report written by juniors. Nor is it unusual for similar changes to take place between the submission of a proposal and the start of work on a project. The overall effect is something like the 'Peter Principle' – that everyone tends to rise to the level of his own incompetence – even though the precondition for the principle to operate – a rigid hierarchical structure – is absent.

If the rate of expansion is forced by recruiting at more senior levels (buying in talent from other similar groups, perhaps), then the direct danger of watering down the quality of the work may be averted. But as in all spheres this can cause a morale problem, which may also harm the work. The think-tank is at least as sensitive to human relationships as other types of organisation (probably more so, as the next chapter will discuss). The arrival of outsiders to take the newly created project leader roles brings with it the danger of resentment and frustration, and if done several times is liable to cause the departure of analysts who feel themselves passed over and blocked for future promotion.

*

The next stage of expansion is the need to form more than one group when the projects exceed the span of a single group leader. A 'group of groups', however, since it is no longer organised by project, has problems which begin to look more like those which are dealt with adequately in the normal management literature and need not be reviewed here. But it is worth considering the level at which the span of a group leader does get over-stretched.

It is impossible for the group leader to be familiar in depth with every aspect of every project. But to what extent can even his more general grasp be stretched so thin that he can make no technical con-tribution at all and becomes merely an administrator? A practical approach used to be advocated by an old-style works-study manager. This was simply to get together with a different project team to discuss problems at nine o'clock every morning. Assuming a five-day week, this gave him a limit of five projects and this is what he stuck at. While his procedure was questionable, if only on account of its rigidity (it continually had to be modified when teams were out of the head office), it does have a beautiful symmetry. And five projects is certainly within most group leaders' scope (the number being not too sensitive to the size of the projects, since the bigger projects can be expected to have stronger project leaders and to need correspondingly less intervention). But there will be many group leaders who can handle more than this. I remember a feeling of ineffectiveness setting in when handling eight projects, and would suggest that troubles would really start when there were as many as ten. This is probably not so depen-dent on the group leader's capability as one might think, since part of the trouble is the proliferation of administrative problems which it is not feasible to delegate to project leaders.

On the other hand, there are other areas where the capability and flair of the group leader has more bearing on the number of projects he can manage. Part of his role is to sustain enthusiasm and confidence – in a project team, for example, who are flagging through having to live with a difficult and perhaps unsatisfying approach. Again, part of his role is to guide the selection and proper application of specific analytical and problem-solving techniques. Since different techniques may be used in each project, the point at which he is overstretched in this can vary enormously according to his general experience and skills. Another important part of his job is in dealing with the 'political aspects'. The speed with which an individual can sense a political problem and react wisely to it will also be a constraint on group size, for the project which runs from start to finish without such a problem is rare indeed.

That some people are better at managing the work and others better at doing it is clear. That this is an over-simplification is also clear. But I hope to have shown in this chapter that the manager's methods – at least as regards the organisation he sets up – have a far more direct impact on the quality of the work itself than is generally admitted.

3 Human Relationships

'Probably more has been written in recent years concerning the application of behavioural sciences in management, with the least amount of general understanding, than almost any other aspect of management activity.'

Innovations in Management Organisation
(UNIDO, Vienna)

In this chapter I turn from the corporate nature of the group to the personalities of the individual analysts, and consider the human relationships between them and their leaders.

If there is a single character trait which distinguishes the analyst, it is perhaps an intellectual arrogance – a belief that he can solve everyone's problems, including those of his boss – which is probably justified more than in the case of the average man, but to a far lesser extent than he believes.

To describe the ideal analyst is easy. He should have a high I.Q.; be academically brilliant but with an understanding of the limitations of academic methods; have wise judgement based on an understanding of human nature; be widely experienced in the field he is working in plus several others so that he can spot parallel concepts; have a strong imagination and the willingness to break traditions and try new ideas; be fluent in communicating both orally and in writing; have an attractive personality so that people are encouraged to explain their problems openly to him; and have the enthusiasm, persistence and patience to complete his assignments successfully. This paragon probably does not exist. I have certainly not met him.

At a less demanding level we can say that it is at least advisable that he be the sort of character who likes to have an understanding of both the mechanism and the qualitative nature of the world about him. It will help his work if he reads widely and has a range of interests particularly in business, technological and socio-economic fields. He will probably enjoy nagging at a problem or a puzzle until he finds an answer, and it would be nice if he was then prepared to agree that a different answer could be better. He should not be in the habit of taking things at their face value, realising that there are always at least two sides to every argument, and is not likely to be the one who believes that 'one swallow makes a spring'.

In real life any individual will be strong on some points and weak on others. It would be glib to classify too readily, but it is probably true – I am indebted to Eric Williamson for the germ of this idea – that there are either 'applications men', 'systems men' or 'techniques men'. The applications man likes to see a problem in simple terms, solve it quickly and get an approximate solution applied as early as possible. The systems man sees a danger in partial solutions and prefers to take a wider view even though it takes longer and the solution is more difficult to implement; his solution may still be somewhat approximate. The techniques man is dissatisfied with approximate solutions to ill-defined problems and likes to use sharper tools which will allow him, provided his assumptions are right, to arrive at an optimum in at least one section of the problem.

Each of the three has a role and a weakness. The applications man does get things done, but his quick solution in one area may cause harm in areas he had

decided not to look at. The systems man should produce a sounder answer and often bring a new light
to a problem, but he may never reach the end of the
road. The techniques man provides a vital service by
forging sharper tools, but the precise-looking solution
which he fashions with them may be narrowly based
and brittle. Too high a concentration of any one type
in a group or a project may be dangerous – and it can
be reasonably argued that a project team should
contain some of each.

Furthermore, the analyst may have a way of going
about his work which is a product of his character,
and which in isolation may not be at all successful. In
Management and Machiavelli, Anthony Jay points
to two quite different character traits. He adopts a
rather vivid sexual analogy by introducing the idea
of the 'stallion' who 'during creative intercourse'
implants the seed of an idea into the 'mare' who
goes away and nurtures it until the brain-child is
born. There is some truth in this interplay between
two different characters, but the mechanism may not
be as close to his analogy as he argues. What more
often happens in my experience is that there is one
type who is high on innovative sense and low on
persistence, and another who is not very original but
when given an idea is prepared to work on it until he
gets it right. The former is often creative but inaccurate: if left to follow his idea through, the result
is likely to be studded with mistakes and omissions.
The latter has greater tenacity and will keep at it –
perhaps plodding rather slowly to a superficial
observer – until he gets to the point which the inno-
vator could imagine but could not achieve. The
analogy of a bloodhound and a terrier working together to catch a badger is perhaps a better one: the
bloodhound senses the location of the badger's lair

but then gets bored and wanders off, while the terrier, once shown where to dig, keeps at it until he unearths the prey. Whatever analogy is used, be it stallions and mares or bloodhounds and terriers, there is no doubt that both these characters are essential to problem-solving, and the right mix (which is usually two or three terriers to one bloodhound) is to be very much borne in mind by the group leader when building his teams.

In operational research groups and think-tanks it has been traditional to use a multi-disciplinary approach. Teams have been formed from graduates chosen for their intellectual qualities rather than their basic discipline – be it engineering, mathematics, economics, etc. – and it has been found that the resulting mixture performs well. It brings a breadth to the work which can be beneficial. This is not to say that the team performance would necessarily be worse if the mix were homogeneous, but a single-discipline team can be dangerous. With modern operational research syllabuses, the necessity of the multi-disciplined approach has been lessened, since the subject-matter of O.R. training has itself broadened to cover those parts of other disciplines which have been found most relevant. A team composed only of O.R. men can therefore be sufficiently broadly based for some problem areas. But in general the view is still rightly held that some admixture of different disciplines is beneficial.

The typical problem-solving analyst is likely to be competent in mathematics and computing, have some knowledge of business and economics, and be familiar with the more important areas of systems engineering and control theory. In other fields he may rely on the analysts from other disciplines with whom he is working; they will bring in different ways of thinking and of tackling problems and will fill in the gaps in his technical knowledge. But in the course of his early career the problem-solver can do a lot to close some of these gaps for himself and make himself less reliant on outside technical help, by further reading. Where the gaps lie will depend upon the man, the course he followed and the problem area he is working in, but there are two which seem to recur frequently and which deserve special effort in reading.

The first is in the social sciences. This need for more attention to human needs is one of the main themes of this book, and I have sketched in a little of the ground. But there is no substitute for going to original works. It is worth recalling the self-training strategy of a prominent businessman: he decided that to succeed in business he first had to know about people, and for this knowledge he read all the classics he could lay his hands on. This reversion to the classics to gain an insight into human nature is important. Modern works on sociology fill a particular role, but for a deep understanding of human motives and behaviour the man who has also studied the classics has a head start. For example, it is only necessary to read one book of Plato's *Republic* to learn a good deal about human aspirations and how weak the 'ideal solution' of the benevolent city-state may look when applied to real people. While doing this the scientific thinker may also broaden his outlook as he notices how Socrates makes the most sweeping assumptions and the most inconsequential jumps in logic without invalidating the progress of his argument.

A second area which justifies further reading is information theory. Random processes tend to be treated rather differently in each discipline which has to work with them, but it is in the theory of signals in noise that the greatest precision is adopted and the greater appreciation of the statistical processes involved may be gained. As an example, there are several types of problem where the concept of an *ensemble* of signals can be useful, and the ergodic hypothesis (which when true allows the instantaneous values of each signal in an ensemble to provide statistics which apply to the long-term variations of any one of them) is a concept which can strengthen the hand of the analyst in a quite different discipline. There are several such principles in information theory which I have found give a better insight into forms of natural behaviour.

The difference of approach which members of different disciplines bring to a team is not an unmixed blessing. It can cause intellectual disharmony – a lack of belief in the other man's methods, and unwillingness to talk out the difficulty. This usually shows up as a degree of arrogance about his own wisdom and a lack of charity over the other man's. The three types of professional who seem most often to misunderstand each other are those in the quantitative sciences, those in the humanities, and those – economists, statisticians, social scientists – who have to work uncomfortably on the twilight border between the two. Let us call these three 'the engineer', 'the arts man' and 'the economist'.

The engineer sees in himself someone practical, precise, and with a sound understanding of the mechanical and dynamic behaviour of the universe; he tends to think of the arts man – and by implication the economist – as always talking about the problem but never sitting down to describe it systematically with real numbers. Engineers seem to find difficulty in believing that there is as much complexity in a piece of legislation, for example, as in the mathematical description of a mechanistic system, and that the intellectual and logical demands made on the arts professions are equal to those made on his own. The arts man, on the other hand, knows that the world is full of people and feels that if you can solve the problem in human terms you have done the hard part; he has nothing against the engineer, but thinks of him as a technician to look after the nuts and bolts of the problem after he has finished with it. The economist veers backwards and forwards . . . and believes he understands both approaches and can do a better job on each of them.

These tendencies, which when put down on paper are patently shallow, crop up surprisingly often. They can best be combated by fostering within the group a spirit of intellectual charity. This must be a personal task of the group leader, who should try to put across the idea that 'All your colleagues are intelligent men; take their wisdom on trust as well'.

Such lack of charity occurs not only between different disciplines, but whenever analysts who are new to each other start working together, and such new teams may need to go through a sort of running-in period. The effect can be stronger still towards the work done by those outside the group, particularly if they are complete strangers. This is less harmful, of course, and does at least liven up the day: what happier sight than an analyst guffawing over the fatuity of someone else's report, or showing it to his colleagues in amused disbelief. It allows him full rein to his critical powers without the need to be polite, which is a healthy form of relaxation. But it can be most unhealthy if the individual or the group snigger too often over other people's work, and particularly if they begin to believe their superiority. As light-hearted relaxation there is not much harm, but at the end, as they go back to their own work, someone ought to say, to break the spell: 'Ah, well, I expect they're saying the same about our last report.' The implication left hanging in the air then is that they ought to take an equally critical look at their own methods.

This lack of respect for the stranger is partly caused by man's tribal instincts, and it helps in fostering a group identity and a feeling of together-ness. But my ideal analyst has to see deeper and have a more balanced view: he should appreciate that there is normally a good reason for the weaknesses of other people's work, and if the author were present to give the other side of the argument they might be seen not to be weaknesses at all. When the lines of communication are weak, or absent altogether, then the analyst has to make an act of faith about the capability of the other man. When he is acting out his amusement or exasperation he is to that extent thinking less deeply; nine times out of ten a deeper study of the text will reveal that the author had something to say which was more right than wrong. I remember an example of this when the comment of a high-calibre expert on a particular section of text prepared by a stranger was: 'This is either so obvious as to be not worth writing or else so profound that I cannot follow it.' It was quite clear which of these alternatives the writer meant – modesty like this is surely false – but after a further hour of study and argument about the text, it was in fact shown that the thought contained in it was neither trivial nor profound. It was a sound but not dramatically original statement which did contribute slightly to the project. It was, of course, very badly written.

The sad thing here was that the expert had not yet learnt the lesson that people – even strangers – are rarely as foolish as to write down the completely obvious: his superficial comment was due both to a lack of time to puzzle it out and a lack of charity.

Age and seniority problems in this type of group are difficult, and although they look easy to solve, this is a misconception.

The difficulty arises from the intensity of personal contact which analysts experience, which means that they get to know each other's capabilities well. This, coupled with the complexity and lack of settled form of the organisation structure they work in, can lead to an unusual sensitivity to slight mismatches between their relative ages, capabilities and allocated responsibilities.

Superficially, the difficulty appears easy to solve because a problem-solving group can be organised on a 'consultancy partnership' basis – a rather formless association of individuals of different seniority who are able to work together on a project without embarrassment. But this in no way removes the need for a clearly designated project leader, which I discussed in the previous chapter, and the temptation to use the device to by-pass difficult seniority problems has to be resisted. It is quite obvious to the members of the team when deliberate evasion is being used to avoid a difficult promotion decision. A favourite device is to appoint a 'project co-ordinator' instead of a project leader – 'to be responsible for project control, leaving Mr X to continue to be responsible for technical aspects'. I have both used and suffered this device myself and have never known it to solve the problem. The team know what are the normal responsibilities of a project leader, and however carefully prepared a statement ('Mr Y, in view of his experience in . . . which is a vital part of the project, will be responsible for customer contact . . .') it is again transparent: Mr Y is being put in charge of the project.

There is nothing magic to offer here on this age-old problem of seniority, merely a reminder that it exists and has to be faced up to with clear-cut decisions, and not avoided by the particular evasions which are possible in a loosely structured group.

In Chapter 1, I said that one of the main ways in which problem-solving can be improved was in the breadth of thinking about the problem and the need to come to terms with social realities. It is here that youth is usually at its weakest, and younger staff have to be watched to see that they take a sufficiently broad view. It is often difficult to rein back a young analyst who is galloping down the long, narrow path of a new technique and persuade him to slow down to a speed at which he can take in the scenery, but it must be done. The value of getting an overview of the problem should always be emphasised. There may even be the need to teach him the value of, for example, a first skim through a text before settling down to read it thoroughly. He may not have appreciated that he will run out of time before covering the whole ground in depth. I recall the occasion when a vital feature of a computer package was never realised by the team using it until one day a more senior man took a quick look at the problem and, skimming through the manual, found right at the end an additional facility which greatly simplified the programs being developed.

The most junior staff – let us call them technical assistants – who are recruited unqualified (to complete their studies on day-release, for example) raise a different problem.

Technical assistants are introduced into a group for two reasons: partly in a praiseworthy attempt to take an early hand in career formation; but chiefly to do the elementary work which is felt to be a misuse of the time of the fully qualified analyst. The type of work which can cause frustration to the young analyst (who wants to use his recently acquired skills to the full) is the routine analysis of a large mass of records or raw data; the preparation and checking of data prior to passing it to the punch-girls; or the prolonged collection of data in the field.

There is a strong case for persuading the analyst, wherever possible, to do such work himself and manage without an assistant. The benefits are many. He usually learns a lot more about the problem and its environment by doing routine data analysis than may be immediately apparent. Most records contain exceptions, annotations and *mistakes*, all of which give him a better feel for the real situation. Sometimes the work of collecting the data brings him into contact with people or with aspects of the problem that otherwise he would not have thought of looking for. There are the simple virtues of discipline and accuracy which he may not yet have acquired. If he has done this type of work himself he will be better able to understand its problems when it is done by assistants. And finally there is the time taken up in explaining what he wants done, and the supervision and correction later – the usual technical delegation problem.

In this formidable list the latter reason is the most telling. However carefully selected, an assistant can be a heavy burden, reporting back every few hours for fresh instructions, or grinding to a halt and saying nothing. He should never be taken on lightly. But in any project the time may come when the mass of routine does undeniably look like a misuse of professional staff and some solution has to be found. I have generally found it more useful to look elsewhere for temporary aid than to recruit permanent technical assistants for the group.

One such temporary source is the computer department – giving the work to one or two of the keener punch-girls. For what may be boring work for a professional may be an interesting break to the routine in the punch-room. There are often slack periods when such work can be fitted in. In a similar vein, locating junior clerical staff from the accounts department, who are used to doing accurate figure work, can be very effective. I have found such staff remarkably well suited to the work. Another source is the local university, in the form of vacation work for undergraduates, or even in-term work if a project involving the data collection can be set up. And finally, when appropriate, help from the clerical staff of the organisation being analysed not only gets the work done but tends to involve the decision-maker's staff more deeply, which is also good.

Although the technical assistant problem exists, it is wise to watch out for its being exaggerated by the impatience of young project leaders who become exasperated at having to explain anything more than once, or to correct the same mistake twice. It takes some people many years to realise that not everyone can be as quick or accurate as themselves. I remember one such project leader working his way rapidly through three successive assistants before realising that it was his own high standards and lack of tolerance that were at fault.

I shall return in the next chapter to the advantage

of all levels of staff, including the group leader, getting involved in data collection to some extent.

A number of years ago in Japan, D. R. Burls expounded to me the 'principle of the expert'. The Burls principle is simply a corollary to the proverb about a prophet's honour in his own country. It states that to be an expert you merely have to arrive from outside professing to be one. You are never put to a test which cannot be bluffed out; no one is prepared to question the wisdom of an in-house expert once he is so established – it is hardly polite, and it rocks the in-house boat. I have since observed the truth of this several times. Its implication here is the danger of accepting that anyone is an expert until he has proved it and not merely said it. Nor is it enough that he arrives trailing a cloud of glory; his experience in the field at issue may be wide, but it may all be unsuccessful experience. It needs stressing not only because of the peculiar way in which a group can compartmentalise its thinking (until one day it discovers that their so-called expert has not been up to the standard of experts in the outside world), but also since the spurious expert has an easy ride into many organisations simply because of their desire to take the opportunity of comfortably transferring responsibility for at least one specialty to a single pair of shoulders.

I have pointed to the need for the members of a cell to talk out their problem until they agree. There will be disagreements, but the vast majority of them can be resolved if pursued patiently enough. On the other hand there are some individuals who are not prepared to talk out a disagreement, and others with whom the effort would be wasted. One would hope that neither of these would be found in the younger members of the group, but this is unfortunately not true, since even junior staff can have a dogmatic bias, and unless they have been treated correctly early on, by the age of thirty they may display all the rigidity more usually associated with those nearing retiring age.

By correct treatment I mean persistently bringing home to the dogmatist that his view may be only one of several, and that each should be examined. This reconditioning will probably spread over a number of issues and many months; it can certainly not be done quickly. And each issue will take time, since when a man is dogmatic but mistaken, his view is usually founded on a broadly-based interlocking structure of experience and reasoning which cannot be toppled lightly. The greatest mistake is to think that five minutes of clear-cut argument is sufficient to do the job; this will make the dogmatist uncomfortable, and although he may agree with the new argument superficially, he is likely to revert to the old one as soon as he leaves the room. His supporting structure remains untouched, and thus the new argument will fade. What is needed is the patience to examine this supporting structure in detail.

There is another type of analyst who may feel like a thorn in the side of the team, but whose needling is best suffered because it does more good than harm to the final quality of the research. He is the man who seems to be for ever worrying about objectives. He will be found, months after the project has started and the rest of the team are quite satisfied that they know where they are going, questioning whether the aims of the project have been properly defined. Invariably they have not: it is rarely possible to be absolutely precise when setting up this type of project. There is usually a gradual evolution of the aim as the ground is surveyed, discussion takes place, and it is seen what is practicable as well as desirable (setting objectives is, like politics, the art of the possible). And so the objectives man goes on needling.

But this needling is valuable. There are generally enough enthusiasts around who want to get started and get something done, so producing a tendency to gloss over the precise objectives, and in correcting this he serves a useful purpose. (Sometimes the problem itself is one of re-examining the fundamental objectives of some activity and the whole team has to put on this particular hat; this will not bring our objectives man to the fore, though, since his worrying is a character trait rather than a methodological approach, and in this case he is more likely to be found worrying about the precise objective of studying objectives.) To make the most use of him it pays to give him the goal-setting aspect of the study as a specific responsibility, but with one proviso: the goal-setting is to be done *as the work proceeds*, not as a detailed preliminary. This proviso is essential, both to prevent hold-ups and to achieve the gradual transition mentioned above. As he may not like it and may continue to point out the impurity of the approach, the project leader – or the group leader if necessary – may have to bear the weight of his continuous disapproval on their shoulders.

This call for purity of approach is a particularly strong trait of a further type – the man who always refuses to compromise. It is characteristic of youth, who normally grow out of it. But when an individual shows signs of not growing out of it as he approaches his late twenties, say, then a special effort is needed to try to make him more flexible. This can demand the same prolonged and tactful handling which we accorded the dogmatist.

For purity of approach, homogeneity of methodology, precision of logic, can all be pursued too far. In some fields of research they may be a virtue, but they will not necessarily give very good solutions to real-life problems. I shall be discussing the spurious precision of some methods of analysis in Chapter 6, but here the point is that even on the occasion when pure methods are known to give precise quantitative answers, their single-minded pursuit can swallow up too many resources and at the same time deprive the project of the richness of texture which comes by taking any opportunity to use whatever method comes to hand, whenever it will give most benefit. Such a pragmatic approach is likely to give more acceptable and more robust solutions, and it is this message which has to be put across to the younger staff. It must not, of course, be an excuse for amateurism, absolving the team from employing the more advanced 'pure' quantitative techniques whenever they have a role to play.

Another character type whom I should mention in this short review is the man who keeps reporting back. In business organisations it is often considered that the span of reporting time is related to the degree of delegated responsibility; spans of one week are considered very short and indicate a trivial degree of delegation; spans of several months are common. In the problem-solving group the best work is done when there is much more frequent contact, and in the next chapter I shall be arguing for even formal meetings to be held every fortnight or so. But what are we to do with the man who, as encouraged by the democratic nature of the group and the 'ever open door' policy of its leaders, keeps reporting back daily

– almost hourly? He is probably an enthusiastic type who is inclined to come back only an hour after a previous discussion brandishing a new diagram: 'Have a look at what I've done!' This can be rather endearing, but also rather disruptive, and the trait itself is worth a little thought.

I believe that his type of behaviour stems from the fundamental human need for contact, not from a lack of ability to accept responsibility. The individual feels a little lonely in his work and wants to share it with someone. So if he keeps coming back too often, the simple remedy is to give him more intellectual contact *within* the team. It will probably be found that he was working on his own and he is the wrong type to do so.

Of course, a group leader who feels that his staff are always interrupting him should ask himself whether he has his priorities right. Is what is being interrupted making as great a contribution to the group's work as the interruption itself? Again, might it not be better to consider taking the mountain to Mohammed and going to call on the analyst *before* he reappears? Such a neighbourly visit will do more good to the lonely man than several barely tolerated visits by him to the group leader's office.

This principle of dropping in on the analysts for a chat about their work is important. I remember a group leader who used to spend a good deal of time nearly every day simply making his way round from one desk to the next, with no special questions in mind and no expectation of a progress report – just keeping in touch, hearing about an interesting development the analyst cared to tell him about, possibly discussing a technique and making a suggestion. This has always seemed to me – I was on the

receiving end at the time – an excellent example to
follow.

On occasion it will be found advisable to include
in the project team a member chosen for his practical
knowledge rather than his analytical skills. He can
bring a great deal of strength to the team by making
sure that their assumptions are soundly based and
that their conclusions are realistic, but for his capabilities to be fully exploited he has also to be drawn
into the more systematic and logical side of problem-
solving. He will most probably already have formed
judgements on the main issues before he joins the
project, and most of his opinions are likely to be
broadly correct. The difficulty is to get him to state
the foundation for these opinions logically. This can
sometimes seem like getting blood from a stone, needing much patience and frequent springing to a blackboard. A good approach is to try to construct a simple
diagrammatic representation of the practical man's
belief and its foundation.

Out of such a discussion the analyst always hopes
that the greater depth of examination will bring to
light either a fundamental fallacy in the 'obvious
relationship', or at least a new way of looking at it
which clarifies the issues. It may be, for example, that
the practical man has been trying for years to convince people that he is right, but that until the analyst
took his argument apart and re-assembled it properly
it was not plausible.

In the last chapter I concluded that if a group is
to expand it is best for it to be in units of one project
at a time. But often this is not practicable, and a
project team itself has to be expanded after the project has started. When this happens there is a real

danger of damaging the quality of the work unless sufficient time is set aside for indoctrinating the new man. If he is an old member of the group, this should be only a question of catching up with the particular thinking on that project, but if he arrives from outside, a good deal of time may be taken up before he is reoriented to the team's own way of communicating and thinking. There will be problems of vocabulary and differences of technique which have to be ironed out. It is wise for the project leader to go a good way along this road in private before letting the differences emerge at a more general project meeting, for two reasons. Firstly, to save time, because the discussion is likely to raise again old project difficulties which have already been satisfactorily overcome, and it will not be productive to go through it all again with the whole team. Secondly, because during these introductory sessions the new man often appears in a bad light: he looks slow on the uptake compared with others who are familiar with all the concepts involved, which is unfair. It is only natural on his part to try hard to make a favourable impression, and this may lead him to display less wisdom than usual, or to lay claim to more expertise than he really has. Unless he is a taciturn type who is content to sit and listen, the end result of throwing him into a detailed project discussion too early can be a partial destruction of his professional image.

A similar problem can occur in technical discussions between the group leader and junior staff, when the former's wider grasp of the subject can lead him to go much too fast. When he is suggesting a technical approach, for example, he may sketch it out so that the analyst just about follows him, or thinks he does, and then leaves the room with the concept evaporating fast; ten minutes later he would desperately like to go back and query one or two points, but is stopped by the need to avoid looking rather foolish. I remember finding myself in this position sufficiently often for me to form the habit of grabbing all the scraps of paper on which the discussion had been conducted – even as they were being screwed up and consigned to the waste-paper basket – in order to bear them away for more leisurely examination. The lesson is simple: patience, and making sure that the other has fully understood, even if this takes 'valuable' time.

A good social atmosphere is clearly essential in much of the management problems I have discussed. Contact between staff at *ad hoc* technical discussions, and the formal progress meetings discussed in the next chapter, both help to create this atmosphere. But they need to be reinforced by group meetings which the group leader should hold from time to time. These should be called quite independently of project requirements, and their purpose is chiefly to foster a feeling of group identity, with a secondary purpose of passing on information which junior staff in particular would not get otherwise.

Group meetings can follow the pattern of any good manager's occasional get-togethers: introducing new recruits, reviewing the general direction in which the group's work programme is evolving, discussing administrative problems, mulling over interesting technical developments, and from time to time asking along senior members of other departments to talk about their work. The meeting must be informal and democratic.

A fault which I have noticed wherever such meetings are planned is too ready a surrender to the temptation to postpone them. So many people with so many urgent tasks push aside the group meeting with its non-urgent business. This is very bad, since it tends to destroy just that morale which the meeting was intended to build up. A meeting which is postponed lightly is a meeting downgraded in significance, and this hits below the belt at staff who were psychologically dependent on such meetings. Wanting to belong is sometimes described as the primary psychological need. So the rules should be: regularity – every two months, for example; a three-line whip to attend; and no cancellations.

This chapter is concerned with human relationships, so let me end it by pointing out again the human relationship which probably matters most – that which affects implementation.

The analyst can try as he will to keep the human element out of his problem when he is planning a project, but it will be impossible to avoid it cropping up again during implementation. It follows that for successful implementation any important human problems should be built into the problem itself as factors to be tackled, not left on the side-lines as nagging nuisances which will either prevent his solution from being given a proper hearing, or will lead to its failure if it is introduced.

For example, take the case of designing a new information and control system. In proposing a revised method by which decisions are to be reached and corrective action taken, the analyst is likely to be pitchforked into the middle of conflicting departmental ambitions and power struggles. One approach is to make the solution independent of such conflict by designing a decision structure which has its own watertight procedures irrespective of which department the decision centres are located in (in fact, in some environments this may be the only way, since the structure may be changing so rapidly that there will have been a departmental reshuffle before the study is finished). An independent information system overlay like this will never be easy to design, of course, but is sometimes possible. But when it is simply not feasible, then the second approach is to set about understanding the individual departmental ambitions and the personal motives of the chiefs – not in order to raise the hands in horror and then submit a report recommending harmony, but to design a system which will be feasible in the environment in which it has to work. Compromise with the ideal in order to accommodate peculiarities of the personalities involved, plus elasticity in the face of the probable future shifting of responsibilities, is the most likely to lead to successful implementation.

There will be analysts who consider all this most devious, who refuse to give recognition to the effects of organisational manœuvring. While this is very praiseworthy from a moral standpoint, it does not help the solution. If the man really feels committed to the implementation of his technical recommendations, then he must realise that some of the steps towards it involve decisions by human beings. And human beings cannot help viewing recommendations in the light of the effect on their own positions. Unless he is specifically asked for an 'academic best solution', the solution put forward by an analyst who refuses to take account of the politics is likely to become rapidly ineffective.

4 Effective Control

In the preceding chapters I have called for an attempt to raise the standard of the work by a broader approach, allied to a more persistent probing for realism. I have suggested that this is more likely to be achieved by calmly and systematically setting aside enough time to argue each point to a conclusion. But to adopt this measured pace and to stay within the confines of available resources demands a compensating increase in productivity. The effort needed to do higher-quality work can only be found by cutting out waste and using each man-hour to the full. This is the object of project control.

Effective project control does not just mean drawing a PERT diagram. Systematic planning and progressing is important, but it must be allied to a good technique of directing the way the work is done and of controlling its quality. In the two succeeding chapters I shall be discussing in particular the quality of the thinking; here I want to consider how to direct a project in a way that will produce the maximum useful work output from the minimum number of staff. This can serve as our definition of productivity, provided there is emphasis on the word 'useful'.

Productivity is not achieved here by working at a high tempo. This may produce the illusion of progress, but the reality may be that the precious man-hours being poured into detailed work could be more productively used in distilling a little wisdom.

Time and again it has been demonstrated that in the intellectual sphere crash projects produce worse answers. If there is a fixed quantity of resources – a given level of funding to solve a problem – then fewer people working for longer will always be more productive than more people working faster. This principle is repeatedly cast aside as the decision-maker needs a quick answer (or thinks he does) and applies the pressure. And yet when you consider the nature of the work it is really quite obvious. Imagine a team trying to solve a difficult crossword puzzle; who could imagine that six men working on it for ten minutes would complete as much as two men working on it for half an hour? (It is no use an awkward reader pointing out that in the six-man team we are more likely to have one crossword genius who will finish the whole thing in ten minutes, because effective control would have meant knowing your men in advance and putting the genius on it alone.)

In research and development in the physical sciences and technology, Beattie and Reader consider that 'a project can be performed at a number of different rates, each consistent with the research strategy, but each having a different cost'. This must assume that the goals will be achieved equally well at any speed and that the only thing that changes is the cost. This certainly does not hold for intellectual problem-solving. Here not only the cost goes up as the pace is forced, but the quality of the answers goes down. The main reason is that the R. & D. project can usually be given clear-cut goals against which the achievement of the project can be measured, while the problem-solving project usually cannot.

Our group's task is rather like cooking a meal. The cook can avoid wasting time, but once he has cut out the waste then there is a natural speed, and any attempt to speed up further is likely to make the final product less palatable. A problem is like a Hungarian goulash – the slower it cooks, the better the result. What we have to avoid in project control is any time-wasting by the cook, who may use up the time available in the wrong way, so that even when on the face of it there is ample time, the meat still comes out tough.

There have been cases, particularly in the United States, where a crash programme has been successful in delivering the goods, but it will usually be found that these were allied to very high staff levels and enormous cost. There is little evidence of a reasonable level of productivity, and indeed a frequent characteristic of such projects is that they tend to crystallise into several teams working in parallel since they are impossible to control. In *Corporation Man*, Anthony Jay argues that this form of natural structuring is caused by the need for a large body of men to break up into units of about ten, as a throwback to tribal hunting instincts. And in these ten-groups the major achievement is being made in only one of them. In the crossword puzzle example this form of crash project would be equivalent to putting so many in the team that there really *would* be a genius among them.

In a lower key, the approach of putting more than one team to work independently has some merit when the problem is of extreme importance and when the decision-maker has no special confidence in one particular team. This may result in sounder answers, but not in faster projects. If at the same time the project duration is adequate, then this

approach will improve the prospect of a good conclusion. But when the money is limited, the case for
splitting it between parallel teams is very weak unless
the decision-maker really distrusts all of them. A
single team, well co-ordinated and with an imaginative approach, given all the available resources, will
generally produce a better result. If it is felt that one
team, although best from most angles, has a gap in
their expertise, then it should be possible to find a
way of co-opting a specialist from elsewhere to plug
the gap.

I recall an occasion when I was in charge of one of
the two teams (in different organisations) who had
been allocated the same problem, when the decision-
maker admitted that he knew in his heart which was
the stronger team but simply could not bring himself
to put all his eggs in one basket. Both teams were
desperately low on staff as the result.

A device which sometimes has attractions in problems concerned with technological innovation is to
set one team looking for the simple solution and
another looking for the sophisticated solution, keeping the two teams completely independent. The latter
team may be given the more resources, and will probably be expected to have additional skills. This may
seem systematic, but I have been on both ends of it
and have found it frustrating and probably unpro-
ductive. Certainly, it does nothing to avoid the
wasteful duplication of data collection and basic
thinking which doubling up always produces, and it
also introduces constraints which hinder both teams.
The team given the simple role is led to feel a little
like a poor relation, and when they get a good idea
may not have the freedom to develop it; the dividing
line is so uncertain that each of them may leave the
middle-of-the-road solution unexplored; and the

team given the 'sophisticated' role fear that they will develop a professional reputation as fanciful idealists, and also have to work under the cloud of knowing that their solution is unlikely to be implemented. A group leader will be well advised to refuse either role and to press for freedom of approach whoever else is working on the same problem.

The use of different approaches by the *same* team is a different matter. This form of parallel working, when co-ordinated, can be extremely powerful. Here it is quite legitimate to adopt the simple/sophisticated polarity, since both cells see what the others are doing. It may be a question of putting one cell on using one technique and a second on a different technique, since neither is expected to be fully satisfactory on its own. Moreover, when a new technique is to be tried by a team for the first time, it will be wise to employ the older technique in parallel with the new. The essential ingredient here is the feedback between the two cells. It will be found that each approach feeds the other: with a view of the problem which is slightly different; with a different form of data analysis which in the event proves more useful; with a partial conclusion from one team which just nicely supplements one from the other – the approach is rich in pattern and serendipity (see Chapter 5). It can be useful if the different approaches form a hierarchy: for example, one operating at a global level in general terms and the other providing more detail.

I do not propose to suggest a systematic sequence of the stages of problem-solving, as this has been done many times and there seem to be as many codifications of the steps involved as there are authors. The broad stages of problem definition and objectives,

description of the system and its environment, generation of solutions and their assessment, are sufficiently
clear to all working in this field. To try to spell them
out as a clear-cut succession of detailed steps is
artificial and dangerous, as I shall show.

There must, of course, be a project plan, and it
must set up a task structure which can be controlled.
But I have never known control by a branching network of conceptually connected intellectual activities
to be successful or even genuine. The genuine need is
to set up at the start of the project a small number of
milestones or key points of progress which are sufficiently concrete that it will be possible to notice when
they have passed. And even this is not easy.

Four or five milestones are often enough. They will
vary from project to project, but could look like this:

A. The point at which the main boundaries of the
   problem have been defined and agreed with all
   concerned.
B. The point at which a definite commitment is
   made on the main analytical techniques which
   are to be used.
C. The point at which no significant further collection of descriptive data takes place.
D. The point at which no further significant thinking takes place.
E. The point at which the final solution has to be
   presented.

It will not escape notice that I have had to qualify
each milestone except the last with the adjectives
'main' and 'significant'; the milestones are always to
some extent blurred, but not so much that they lose
their value as control points.

In between these milestones, activities should be
progressed in parallel rather than in sequence,

according to a principle of maximum feedback similar to that I described in the 'funnel diagram' of Chapter 1. This is a basic principle of the work which is often smothered by attempts to apply PERT and critical-path methods to intellectual activity for which they were not intended.

An example may be useful. Let us take a fairly typical project which starts with a literature survey to find out what has already been done; having assimilated this, there has to be an assessment of available techniques; after choice of techniques there has to be analysis and application of the techniques; then conclusions have to be drawn; finally a report must be written. (I protest that I have not gone back on my refusal to spell out the steps of problem-solving – this sequence is in no way intended to be standard. It merely serves as an illustration.)

Given this method of conducting the project, it is tempting to draw a diagram such as Fig. 2.

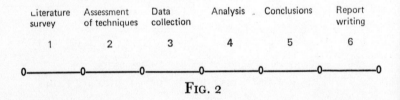

FIG. 2

With a little more realism, since it is suddenly realised that very little time seems to be available for each activity, a little overlapping is brought in, as shown in Fig. 3.

This is a step forward, acknowledging that some basic data collection can be done before it is precisely decided what techniques will be used to analyse it; that conclusions can start to be drawn before all the analysis is complete; that report-writing can start as

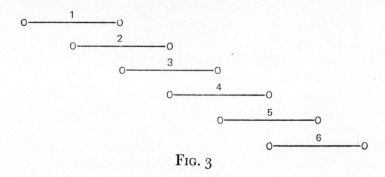

F<small>IG.</small> 3

soon as the conclusions start rolling off the production line, and so on.

It is still not good enough. Who can believe that from the day he is first faced with the problem and before he has unearthed the first literature, the analyst is not already assessing techniques in his mind? Again, if the report is to be a good one it will need to refer to work done in every stage, basing itself on technical notes produced en route. Thus one can consider report-writing to be continuous throughout the project.

As the work progresses and the team make contacts, their horizons of literature search will widen; also, some literature will arrive very late although ordered early; thus fresh literature will come to hand quite late in the piece and it would be folly to ignore it. During the analysis, data will be found to be inadequate or incorrect and a fresh round of data collection will be needed even after much of the analysis has been done.

And so we could go on. This overlapping is impossible to define precisely but it is far greater than is usually admitted. Very often the overlap is so great that there is little point in drawing a diagram to show it (although it is fashionable to draw dotted lines leading into an activity to show that they actually start before the diagram says so, as if this helped), and so we are left essentially with nothing but a list of actions to be taken, each to be set in motion from the word 'go'.

Clearly, this is a far cry from effective control, particularly as we have only been considering a small project consisting of one intellectual cell. For if there are several cells, each devoted to a particular area of the problem (for example, one on social aspects, one on technological feasibility, one on costing and pricing), then there is a separate, and broadly similar, sequence of overlapping steps for each of them, together with several logical interconnections between them. Surely now there is a case for controlling the project with a network?

Again the answer is no. (We shall see in a moment that logical network diagrams have a part to play. But not this part.) The principle of overlapping and maximum feedback within the project applies even more strongly now. How can work on feasibility be done without an idea of costs, and how can costing be done without knowing what the shape of the technical solution is? We have the usual chicken-and-egg situation which is soluble only by doing a little of everything, and doing it from the start. Never mind the apparent logical impossibility of starting one activity before another on which it depends is complete: this is a conceptual formality only. *Ça n'existe pas.*

The clinching reason behind this heresy is that analysts are more productive when they are permitted to split their thinking and let several lines of reasoning germinate and ripen over a longer period, even if several remain only in the background while they work overtly on one activity in particular. By contrast, if (owing to an excess of strict project planning) a man is shown that he does not have to start work on a certain aspect until such-and-such a later time, then he probably will not. As a result his thinking is put in a strait-jacket: he could have had a rough stab at it very early and kept it in mind for much longer. Discouraging such preliminary thought is bound to make the analyst that much the more narrow-minded when he is working on the other activities 'which come first'. This must be a bad thing.

There is a similar principle which governs time-sharing between projects in order to give each as much time as possible. Whatever the size of project, each analyst needs time to set in motion the sources of his information, carry out discussion, let serendipity play its part free of charge, and generally to let one aspect of the problem mature while working on a different one. This suggests that he should split his time between tasks. In a large project there is no problem; there will be enough tasks for each analyst to split his time between several of them and still be dedicated to the project. But with smaller projects such a natural rate of advance may mean that the level of effort has to be a part-time one. Where the group's programme of work permits it, it is then a good deal more effective for an analyst to work on the small project in parallel with a bigger task, over a substantial period.

For example, during the course of a two-year, five-man project, several very much smaller tasks were undertaken – tasks each needing in total only about one man-month of effort. But because each analyst had a year or so in which to fit this effort, the resultant quality of thought was very much higher than it would have been if he had waited until a convenient point to interrupt the main task, carried out the minor one in one month, and then gone back. Such extension in time will mean that the answer comes later and may cost marginally more, of course, but the improvement in the quality of the answer will normally make the approach very much worth while. There may be a need for something of a compromise with the principle that a team can do better work when it is dedicated full-time to a project, but the balance is clearly in favour of time-sharing under these circumstances.

In one group I remember, a tradition had grown up of writing a detailed layout and contents list of the final report – down to individual sub-paragraph headings – before starting the project. This caused some amusement to new arrivals, but it did not escape notice that later on the new arrivals had adopted the same habit. They had appreciated a merit in the approach which I believe supports the case for parallelism. This was a group specialising particularly in a fairly narrow field of work where the analysts were not faced with brand-new problems, so the approach was less absurd than it sounds, but it confirms the point at issue. What it achieved was what parallel planning is trying to achieve: to place in front of the analyst at the start of the project a panorama of all the ground he will have to cover, and to authorise him to have a look at any part of it and do some thinking about it as early as he likes. (This 'write the report first' approach is not often to be recommended, since it can prevent flexibility of thinking and originality; the temptation to decide the report layout should normally be resisted until about half-way through the project.)

The parallel approach to a certain extent has the nature of a progressive completeness. Taken to its limit, it would be possible to halt the project at any time and find that the whole study had been done – but that the longer it was allowed to run, the deeper the analysis and the better the conclusions. Problem-solving is more like the painting of a picture than the painting of a house.

But the progressive completeness has to be pinned down at a few points, otherwise it becomes formless, uncontrollable jelly. Even the portrait painter has to decide when to change from sketching-crayon to oil-paint. The control points are our milestones. The shape of a project plan is then like that shown in Fig. 4.

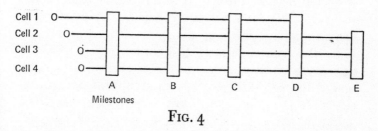

FIG. 4

Notice that in this there is no pretence that any activity is dependent on any previous activity, which is why I have drawn the milestones an unconventional shape. There is, on the other hand, a strong intention that the separate lines of activity are kept in step with each other by trying to make sure that each of them reaches a given milestone at the same time; this is a major concern of this form of control. The only sequential structure is that one or two tasks must be started a little earlier, and one or two finish a little earlier.

Conventional project networks are unfortunately still fashionable, and many decision-makers demand their use. A searching review of such methods and their value is given by Beattie and Reader, who concede something of my distrust but conclude that on balance their value is proven – for technological work, at least. But trying to solve an intellectual problem according to a connected network, however well thought out, is trying to paint a colour picture of a chameleon. The logic of the connections can change almost daily as a new point of view arises, new information comes to hand, simpler ways of doing things are thought of. A simple experiment which proves the point is to ask two people to draw a network diagram of the same intellectual project (at any time – either before, during or after completion of the project). The fact that they will be found to have drawn widely different diagrams brings home the point that controlling the project according to either one of them must put an unreal constraint on the team. In my experience such diagrams are rarely referred to after their initial purpose has been achieved (generally of blinding someone with science). Some project leaders will admit if pressed to using a simple bar-chart rather like my last diagram to do the actual control, but a detailed project network to carry into each formal meeting.

There is no need to be so underhand. Luckily the conventional network is still required (and can still be used for illicit purposes if desired), but in a different role: not as a method of active control, but as an early working tool for determining all the different tasks which go to make up the whole, and the different avenues of analysis which will be required. That is, as a way of examining the extent and scope of the study during the planning stage – as a means of getting the initial panoramic view.

In such a planning network the project leader can

be as fanciful as he likes, and can insert as many conceptual connections as he can handle. In fact, this diagram is a handy way of giving form to the early brainstorming sessions discussed in the next chapter. Since the network is not going to be a rod for anyone's back, there is nothing against it becoming a large white elephant as more and more individuals spring to the blackboard and add to it. White elephants simply cannot be used as rods.

Some simplification of such a brainstorming diagram will be needed, of course. After the meeting the project leader can sit down and bring a little more system and sanity into it. It may then take on a second purpose – to show how groups of similar activities can be formed and allocated to individual project cells.

Monitoring and controlling progress can only be done successfully at regular progress meetings, of a semi-formal nature. Unfortunately there is a great deal of confusion over the value of meetings, whether formal or not. One school of thought considers all time spent in talk as a distraction and a waste of time. Another believes that meetings should be held whenever there is anything to discuss and that moreover they should be open-ended. Perhaps this controversy would be resolved if each meeting were to be made more effective; in my experience not nearly enough attention has been paid to this.

The first half-hour or so of most project meetings is enjoyable. The team, stimulated by an interruption of their desk work, can relax and listen to fresh opinions. A simple review of progress is not too demanding. After a while, however, serious problems are raised which affect more than one team member. If these are to be discussed constructively they will take time. The depth of discussion increases and now communication problems arise. It is discovered that words are being used differently; the other man explains himself badly; someone misses the point. It all starts getting rather laborious.

At this point some people get cold feet. They suddenly see a complete half-day stretching in front of them, and the prospect appals them. So a placebo is introduced – shelving the problem 'until Henry has done some more work on it', or asking 'John and Henry to get together on this and circulate a short note on their conclusions' – and the meeting is rapidly wound up. The man who called the meeting has apparently decided that the cumulative loss of working time of all those present outweighs the advantage of their staying to thrash out the problem. But inevitably his view is coloured by the memory of what is waiting for him in his in-tray, and also by a form of sensitivity which says: 'I really cannot keep all these good people sitting here much longer; I called them together and they are holding me responsible for using up their valuable time.'

Being coloured, this view is highly suspect. In fact, the closure move is often made just when the team are beginning to get their teeth into a problem and starting to talk sense to each other, thus at last putting some unity of thinking into their parallel lines of activity (which is what turns a group of experts into a team). Since the preliminaries have probably achieved little, closure at this point really does ensure that time has been wasted.

There are two solutions: either to go on for the time it takes to reach a constructive advance in thinking, or to pass the problem to a subcommittee – immediately. It is no use letting the subcommittee reform at their own convenience: after a day's delay they may very well take a different point of departure.

The best way of forming such a smaller discussion group is to stay put and invite anyone who feels that he is not fully involved to drop out. The fact that few will want to do so tells its own story.

According to Robert Townsend, 'some meetings should be long and leisurely; some should be mercifully brief'. This is right as far as it goes, but it does not go far enough. Whether or not they are long, few of the meetings we are discussing will be by any means leisurely. The meeting should have been called to cover specific topics and the order of the day should be hard and continuous thinking, slowed down only by the difficulties of communication itself.

Concentration is needed. The art of concentrating for long periods should be a basic skill of a good analyst, and the exhaustion it may cause is a rigour he must accept. The world does not owe him a living, and he cannot reasonably expect to be paid a good salary for doing work that he enjoys unless he is prepared to suffer a little for it. This concentration may last all day (to be sure, short breaks every hour or two boost energy) and the project or group leader may have to force the pace all day. This is hard work.

The point of discussing a question at all is that by putting together two or more sets of information and opinion and massaging them, what emerges will be sounder, wiser or possibly something new. Indeed, as Colin Cherry points out, every single utterance during a conversation changes the hearer's state of belief about his world – 'strengthening some hypotheses, weakening others'. So the most fruitful discussions are those that take place between people who hold a view but are willing to change it. It is a strength, not a weakness, when as a result of hearing a contrary view and examining it an analyst shifts his position. Anyone who is heard to object: 'But half an hour ago you said . . .' has missed the point. A shifting view-point is the hallmark of a useful discussion, and anyone who never shifts is making the meeting that much the more ineffective.

The need to carry on until agreement is reached might well frighten some people. But remember that we are dealing here with a single project team which has been given the joint responsibility for solving a problem. A majority report and a minority report are out of place. And in fact a meeting of minds – a consensus view – can be achieved far more often than may be thought possible if the two parties adopt the approach of arguing it out point by point and with determination to reach the truth.

But of course there will be times when the consensus is impossible. This will happen when the arguments stem from roots of differing human values, rather than on facts or logic. There are several fundamental human values on which analysts have a right to disagree. The most frequently occurring, which no argument is likely to resolve within the time-span of a project, are: the relative virtues of free enterprise and of a planned economy; the virtue of discipline as opposed to a liberal attitude; the degree of certainty required before a guess can be accepted, and the whole question of when a risk is justified; the virtue or otherwise of centralisation; and the relative merits of modern technology compared with the simple life. It might be thought that this list is long enough to kill all possibility of agreement, but it is surprising how many problems can be thrashed out without getting down to this bedrock of value-judgement.

Progress meetings need to be fairly frequent and preferably regular. The most suitable interval between them depends on the type of project and the calibre of staff, but less so than might be imagined. At one extreme the weekly meeting has in my experience invariably been too often, even with short projects. It is altogether too distracting and time-wasting, since if the meeting is to be a review of the progress of all activities the same ground will be repeatedly covered (and if the activities are divided into groups and only one group taken each week, a form of Parkinson's Law creeps in and each will still occupy the best part of half a day). At the other extreme, with an interval of more than four weeks the problems for examination and the decisions to be taken build up until even the dedicated meetings-man may start to run out of steam. And if the interval is too wide, time has to be spent on each occasion getting everyone back on the same wavelength. A progress meeting every two or three weeks seems to work well in nearly every case.

At a progress meeting a quick look should be taken at each line of activity. This keeps all team members on their toes and keeps them contributing. It seems less useful in this type of work for project control to be by 'exception reporting' where a subject is only raised when there is a problem. There is really no good yardstick of performance against which to locate the exceptions. The lines of activity can form useful headings for the structure of the meetings and also for the brief notes which should be written about any decisions taken. Detailed minutes are only a burden, but brief notes form a very useful record of the development of the project methodology which can be valuable later, as well as a means of placing actions.

A main preoccupation of the meeting will be to watch the approaching date of each milestone (one imagines several progress meetings to each milestone, although there could perhaps be only one), and to try to adjust the rate of progress in each so that they all reach the milestone in step and up to schedule. This makes for a well-balanced project. Speeding up or slowing down is achieved partly by the amount of pressure applied, partly by cutting corners, and partly by reallocation of staff. A project well under way gains an understanding of how much work is involved in each line of activity which could not have been well judged at the start, and a rearrangement of responsibilities is quite legitimate.

When a line of activity is lagging behind and it looks difficult to bring it into line without cutting corners too dangerously, there is a further possibility. This is what we may term the pick-up method.

In an earlier chapter I pointed out that the most experienced member of the group can often make much more progress in a short time than the more junior analysts. This can be capitalised on. The climate must be fostered where the leader can without embarrassment take the badly lagging activity under his wing and, by giving special attention to it, can pick it up and move it quickly forward.

The pick-up is fairly commonplace when it comes to report-writing, as discussed in Chapter 7, but tends not to be used enough during the course of a project, often because group leaders allow themselves to be too busied with other tasks. (But when the crunch comes and a weak chapter is found in a draft report which is running up against its deadline, it is remarkable how the time can be found.) It is a great pity to leave the pick-up until the last minute when there is very little time for a thoughtful contribution; the operation may become merely cosmetic. This may of course be due to ignorance rather than procrastination, since it may not be apparent when an activity is lagging enough to warrant the action. However, the management attitude I have advocated should encourage the members of the team to be honest and realistic about their chances of doing a good job on time.

For it will be a sure waste of resources if anyone sits on a problem and does not ask for help. If there is one single way of raising his team's productivity, it is for the project leader to make sure that this does not happen. Both in his normal day-to-day discussions and in the progress meetings, he can consider it a black mark if any of his team have to admit that they have been stumped for more than twenty-four hours without his knowing. If there is enough mutual help between team members, then each line of activity should progress *at the speed of the team,* not at the speed of an individual. And it should be hammered home to all members of the group that they are judged on progress itself, not on whether they made it without help. Of course, progress achieved by one man alone is more valuable than precisely the same progress by several, but only on the grounds of pro-ductivity, not of *amour propre.*

The pick-up approach may not involve the senior man in overmuch work. It is often possible to examine a problem and within the hour add a new dimension, suggest a new direction, give a simple clarification, and hand the ball back to the analyst. This is not because the senior is a superman. It is because he comes to the problem with a repertoire of tricks of the trade which he can call on, and also with a fresh mind.

This approach is open to the standard criticism that it stifles initiative and fails to let an analyst get into trouble deeply enough to call on his own resources. But this is a luxury which can only be afforded in lines of activity which are not under pressure. It can certainly not be justified in activities which are lagging, or showing signs that they soon will.

At an early stage of the project the team has to reach a reasonable understanding of the environment in which the problem exists. This familiarisation needs to be down-to-earth and practical. As many members of the team as possible should go and get their feet wet or their hands dirty.

Most project leaders will recognise this, but may from time to time be tempted, or be talked into, analysis and model-building without familiarising themselves with the system under study. A prime example of this was the detailed proposal which had been put forward for a maximum-security prison on reclaimed land just off-shore in the Wash. One of the virtues of this was claimed to be that even if a prisoner escaped he could only swim to the shore, which could be easily patrolled. A team was given the task of examining this and other proposals, and as a matter of routine went on a familiarisation visit. Driving round the area with a camera, they soon found that the prison site was not surrounded by sea, but by wide areas of salt-flats which partially filled with water, according to the tide. There were also channels criss-crossing the flats, deep enough to hide an escapee from an army of searchers, and sufficiently washed by the tide to remove the scent and make dogs useless. To make matters even worse, it was discovered by talking to the locals in the nearby pubs that a man could live for weeks on the flats by eating a kind of weed which grew there. It appeared that the design of the prison had been done from a map.

An awful warning: always, without any exception, go and see it, walk over it, talk to people working on it and if possible join them for a week or two to see what working on it is like. The outcome is bound to be a better understanding and a better solution.

Familiarisation may have to extend over several visits, partly because the local staff themselves often need time to get round to providing the descriptive data that they possess. This data may be in their heads, which means that an analyst may have to go over the same ground several times before the local staff give the full answer, but even when it is on paper, the analyst may have to query its existence several times before it is recalled.

Such patience was rewarded when, on the third visit to the accounting department of an old-established institution, the analyst asked yet again whether they were quite sure that they did not have the figures broken down by operating locations rather than by heads of services. Very diffidently, the head of the department said: 'Well, there was that analysis we did two years ago for the Parliamentary Inquiry – I don't suppose you will be interested in that.' And he went to a particular drawer and produced a most complete analysis which saved the team weeks of work. This type of diffidence, which is partly due to a lack of rapport during the earlier visits, is not at all rare.

One of the typical milestones which I mentioned was the point at which the collection of descriptive data is essentially complete. There is a useful way to mark this event, although it involves a good deal of hard work. This is to write a detailed working paper describing the system under study together with current methods of operation and special features which affect the aim of the study. This working paper is bound to contain errors of fact and of emphasis, however much care has been taken to obtain accuracy. This is to be accepted and welcomed, since it is only by setting up such an 'Aunt Sally' and asking the local staff to shoot at it that the misunderstanding in the team's mind will be brought to light. The fact of committing to paper an inaccurate description clearly has its dangers, and its aim must be clearly spelt out to the recipients from the outset. There is certainly no need for apology when errors in the Aunt Sally come to light, since this is what it is for – a catalyst in the familiarisation process. The day on which the resulting comments have all been assimilated is the point when this particular milestone can be said to have been passed.

A project will be the more effective if close attention is paid to paperwork. This means getting into the habit of progressively setting down on paper both the evolution of thinking during the project and the ideas – good and bad – which people have during the course of it.

Noting down good and bad ideas is needed because most people's memory is worse than they are willing to admit. I have often found that during the latter part of a project the same ground is being examined in a discussion as had been covered quite adequately earlier. A simple note of the main points of a discussion can avoid this. For example, in a traffic project, the specific meaning of the 'desirable excess capacity' of a part of the system was being discussed, when someone said: 'Wait a minute – surely we talked about this some time ago, and didn't someone note it down?' And because on this project the documentation was in fairly good order, it was possible to leaf back through a series of technical notes and find that the speaker was right, and that a perfectly good definition *had* been written down, plus the main logic behind it. That particular discussion was able to break up a good deal earlier than had been expected.

When drilling a deep hole through a variety of strata, oilmen find that as the drill penetrates and approaches its goal it deviates so that the final point where it emerges into the oil-bearing rock is not directly below the starting-point on the surface. It deviates for two reasons: because the drill has a bias and will not go exactly vertically unless repeatedly corrected; and because if the oilmen run up against a particularly hard stratum en route they have cunning methods of guiding the drill-bit to avoid it and go for the soft rock.

Problem-solving is very much like this. As the thinking progresses, the concepts and the problem structure will deviate from those set up at the beginning. The point of arrival is not the point of departure. But there is one vital difference where this rather laboured analogy does not hold: the well-head – the location of the starting-point – will have ceased to exist unless it was written down. The analysts are down there with the drilling-head, knowing where they have reached and what their finishing concepts are, but generally with no knowledge of those en route deviations which were due to their own built-in bias, and with only a very hazy recollection of even the deliberate deviations which they chose. This latter ought to worry them. The deviations were made to avoid difficulties, hence they probably involved short-cuts such as simplified assumptions and the abandonment of detailed analysis. Forgetting that these short-cuts were taken leads to misplaced confidence in the conclusions.

The team that has written nothing down on the

way is in real danger. It will seldom have much power of self-criticism and may be deluded into thinking that it has solved a problem which it has only by-passed. It may produce conclusions which, although they are based on a very reasonable approach, are open to easy criticism. And of course, without a record of the deviations and the location of the hard rock, the next project team may spend just as long drilling as the first.

Lack of progressive documentation is one reason for the lack of worth-while case-history reports which is regularly bemoaned by conference organis-ers. To write a useful case-history from scratch at the end of a project requires a prodigious memory and an inhuman lack of personal prejudice. It is unlikely to be very valuable, and it is little use vowing to write it all down once the final report is out of the way, since 'when a job is completed something of greater urgency than documentation will immediately materialise', to quote a wise United Nations report.

The brief minutes recording main points decided at progress meetings do to a certain extent contain a history of project progress, but the main repository will be a series which we may term 'technical notes'. The precise form of these will be a matter of taste, but there are some simple principles.

Whatever the length or style, there should be a single series rigorously numbered. This makes sure that none are later mislaid, and means that there is a simple mechanism for keeping each member of the team informed about the work of the others and for bringing new members up to date. Style is absolutely free. One note can be a half-page list of headings and the next a twenty-page report on a detailed area of work. (The Aunt Sally system description will naturally qualify.) Anything goes, since the notes are for internal consumption only, although until they get the feel of the method some analysts may be diffident about putting their unfinished ideas down on paper.

Unhappily, it is not only the progress documentation which generates paper. In an active project there is a variety of other sources, all equally essential, all proliferating paperwork – so much so that some members of the group may be justified in wondering if things have got out of hand.

This was the view several years ago of a British Army colonel who decreed that in his regiment there would be one paperless day each week. This was a noble concept, forcing officers to leave their desks and go out and do something – anything. But it lasted only a few weeks, fading out luckily before the Quartermaster went mad from frustration. There is a lot to be said for prising analysts away from their desks, particularly when they are studying a problem in an environment strange to them. I have never known a project fail to be strengthened by sending the team to have just one more look at the site of the action.

But in general there is nothing to be feared in a sea of paper provided that it is technical paper, dealing with the real work of the group. Paperwork coming from the administrator's department, on the other hand, is quite a different story. With good supporting services and good secretaries there should be no need for anyone but group or project leaders having to occupy his precious desk-space with an administrative document. A useful device to avoid this is for all instructions, circulars, etc., to be put in a book which all members of the group are encouraged to browse through periodically.

Finally, documentation can play a backstopping

role in the process of communication within a project. Oral communication in discussions and meetings is vital, but with the best will in the world it can still fail, and the results can be serious. Timely documentation passed around the interested members of the team can help to pick up these failures, some of which are the type of mistake which hardly takes place on paper. For example, a team was analysing rail movements; the practical man, who had a feel for tons and densities of cargo, was asked by the analyst building the model for the average capacity of a standard railway freight wagon in cubic metres (to be combined with the cargo densities to get tons). The figure of 20 was given and had been used for some time before the practical man – belatedly – released a brief technical note which he had written much earlier but had hung on to because it had been rather rough. The analyst noticed immediately that it was 20 tons, not 20 cubic metres, and had to repeat a good deal of work. The lesson is clear: technical notes should be passed around as soon as they are written, however rough, *not* after they have been revised and edited. This may be too late.

Much has been written on the subject of cost control. The need for controlling costs even of pure research is by this time clear, but practical ways of doing it are in short supply. And methods which apply successfully to intellectual activity specifically are even more so.

We have already seen the difficulty of setting precise objectives and choosing precise levels of manpower input, so that the work specification has to be kept fairly open at the start of a project. By its very nature, the project will be exploring new ground and will be continually meeting new problems whose solution is more or less germane to the main objective. But to solve every problem that crops up in the course of the work will inevitably stretch the boundaries of the research. Fighting this tendency is not only difficult on psychological grounds (the pioneering element of the work will always be present, and if killed completely is likely to demoralise a good team); it also technically weakens the work – however slightly. There can always be a wide difference of expert opinion as to what is essential to achieving the main goal and what is not.

So in the face of these blurred boundaries, with their tendency to spread, the project leader badly needs a budget to hold on to. And the group leader needs to make sure that the budget is drawn just a little tighter than the project leader finds comfortable, in the hope that it will exert pressure on him not to let the problem boundary expand. But since forces drawing the boundary wider are usually stronger than the will-power to resist them, there is a good probability that the project leader will be inclined to overrun his budget. Adding on a contingency for the unknown is thus prudent, but should the size of the contingency be made known to the project leader? For analysts are human and are bound to act differently when they know that a contingency exists than they would if they knew that there was none.

Some time ago I tried to keep contingencies secret, and went as far as having two separate and detailed project budgets (one for management, and one for the project team), but it was not much of a success. The gaff was always blown by someone. The best approach seems to be to have an openly admitted contingency, but to bring it home to all concerned that they are considered rather less successful when they eat into it. If progress is being monitored, then at any time when overrun is predicted the contingency can be allocated, and the project leader can plan to the end of the work with his new funding; the contingency is then consumed gradually, but if it is all used then there should be more than a hint of failure in the air.

Project situations can be very difficult to retrieve retrospectively. Early corrective action demands frequent and automatic management information showing total commitment against progress achieved. Deviation from the planned rate of spending can then trigger the decision to tackle a new difficulty, by-pass it, or lower the sights of the whole project.

On the other hand, the measurement of progress in problem-solving is wellnigh impossible in any strict sense. Often the closest to progress measurement which we can get is to notice the passing of milestones. It may then be objected that there will be only four or five points of checking progress throughout quite a lengthy project, and this is often true. I have normally found this acceptable, although admittedly making the best of a bad job. (Remember that technical control is being exercised at the more frequent progress meetings; without these, the four or five checkpoints would certainly not be enough.)

For those who insist on something more accurate and who are prepared to work at it there is a stricter method, which looks a little childish perhaps, but which has been applied successfully in some environments. This is to use an intuitive yardstick of completion in each line of activity. At each progress review the analyst responsible is asked: 'How far are you along the road to completing the work?' And he has to answer '50 per cent', '90 per cent', etc. The attraction of this is that it concentrates the analyst's attention on the approaching end of his task so that by watching the rate at which time is running out (usually faster than his rate of completion) he can make the necessary adjustment to his work (usually to cut back on detail). The argument that these intuitive figures can be adjusted to suit the occasion does not hold, since if an analyst says he is successively at 80 per cent, 90 per cent, 95 per cent, 97 per cent, . . . , of completion, then the rate of slowing up his estimates as he hits the deadline shows clearly that something is wrong. Without corrective action, estimates like these show that the project is without doubt going to overrun.

For such a control to work, all concerned have got to believe in its value, and not all teams will be able to support the idea. It may well be worth making the effort to persuade them.

In this chapter I have set out a personal approach to the control of problem-solving projects, and I appreciate that there will be many other approaches. I hope, however, to have shown that although this type of work needs strong control, it is a rather different form of control from that used in some other project fields.

5 Creative Thinking

Mr Paleo: I am fed up with all this logistic – a mechanical game with symbols, and a corruption of all logic. The use of logistic is to me one of the symptoms of the decay of our culture. People do not want to think any more, they just calculate.

Mr Neo: My dear Mr Paleo, I am afraid you have never tried to work out any proofs in logistic, for if you had you could not possibly say such things. Not less but rather more thought is required in our domain, and if we use formalism it is in order to render the tremendous task of thought less arduous, indeed possible.

P. Banks, 'On the Philosophical Interpretation of Logic:
An Aristotelean Dialogue', *Dominican Studies*, III

A realistic approach, a good management climate, an environment conducive to hard thinking, and effective control of progress all matter very much. But what turns a mediocre problem-solving team into one of excellence is the quality and originality of the thinking that takes place.

There are not many problems where traditional methods of approach and standard analytical techniques are satisfactory in themselves. The great majority of problems have some new feature which means that, even if there appears to be a quite suitable standard technique, originality is needed if the solution is to be realistic. Creative thinking, and the ways in which it can be fostered, is the keynote of this chapter.

In the opening pages of this book I discussed the novel solution to a problem in connection with major leaps of originality – complete changes of direction. Much of what follows will help there as well, but I am more concerned here with all the minor ways in which creativity can help along the way towards the solution. The team should always be on the lookout for original improvements, new insights and imaginative short-cuts which advance the project without destroying accuracy.

Perhaps the best exponent of originality is Edward de Bono – the creator of lateral thinking – and it is useful to adopt his own terms: *lateral thinking* as opposed to *vertical thinking*.

There is no real substitute for reading de Bono in the original, particularly in view of his easy style and leisurely pace. But this chapter would certainly not be complete without a summary of his approach.

In vertical thinking logic is in control of the mind, whereas in lateral thinking logic is at the service of the mind. Vertical thinking is digging holes deeper and deeper even though the hole is in the wrong place. Lateral thinking is digging the hole somewhere else. This is reminiscent of my oil-well analogy in Chapter 4, except that the thinking which I described there was vertical with deviations (which is the more usual sort). De Bono would say that instead of this laborious progress there may be an easy way of getting to the oil by starting somewhere quite different.

Experts have a vested interest in vertical thinking, since they are specialised in it – they can dig deeper holes faster.

De Bono does not profess to be able to train people in the art of lateral thinking, but he does give useful techniques which will help them to escape from the strait-jacket of vertical thinking. The first of these is to search for the dominating idea in the problem and expose it so that its polarising influence on thought can be destroyed; or alternatively to distort the dominant idea until it collapses by exaggerating its features.

Abandoning an inadequate hypothesis rather than working on it to make it fit is another technique. Once cast aside, there may be room for a quite new hypothesis. Such shifting of viewpoint is a skill which only seems able to be advocated, not explained. Jenner is quoted: he shifted from why people got smallpox to why dairymaids did not, and came up with cowpox vaccine.

Avoiding the rigidity of words is useful. Describe the problem visually and it may take on a 'plasticity that words may never achieve'.

Looked at in a different way, a problem may no longer exist. This is interesting: to see what happens if the problem is *not* a problem might be introduced as a regular catalyst at the start of a project.

One should not be browbeaten out of the right to doubt an explanation when one cannot offer a better one. This inhibits thought, and is not even logical. Everyone has the right to doubt.

Turning the problem on its head, by reversing some relationship, transferring relationships to different situations, and shifting emphasis from one aspect of the problem to another, are also ways of quickly getting a new way of looking at things.

Instead of classifying things, which introduces too much control for a lateral thinker, and which tends to dissect, the lateral thinker refuses to classify but looks for an overall view – a synthesis.

In lateral thinking, logic is suppressed while the ideas germinate. Logic has to be introduced at some stage to bring discipline to the idea, but not too early or it may kill it. De Bono advocates alternating periods of lateral and vertical thinking to get the best of both worlds, and this seems a powerful piece of wisdom.

Creative thinking can make good use of two other important principles which are by no means confined to lateral thinking. One – the generation of as many ideas as possible, however wild – has been part of the creative scene for many years. The other – serendipity – has become fashionable only recently.

If when digging for potatoes a farmworker turns up some Roman coins when nothing was further from his mind, this is serendipity – the discovery of something valuable by 'happy accident' (from the fable of the Princes of Serendip who were particularly prone to it). This can range from picking up the wrong book and finding that it happens to have just what you were looking for, to finding out that your new next-door neighbour happens to be an expert on a subject which is currently plaguing you. Serendipity has been around a long time, but has only recently begun to be respectable.

People talk of the 'art of serendipity', but in fact the only art is in knowing that it can happen and keeping an eye open for it. There is a resemblance to one of the recipes for sleep: put yourself in the best position and wait patiently for it to happen. This is not a question of rooms full of thinkers waiting passively for inspiration, but rather of analysts taking active steps to make sure that while carrying out one task they are in a position to benefit from anything else which crops us. For example, when deciding whether or not to go and talk to somebody, it may be felt that there is not a great deal of common ground and so it is not worth going to see him just to discuss one point. Wrong. There is the very strong chance that the other man will also have something to say on a quite different point which was not the object of the discussion, but which strengthens the team's work. Again, reading a journal which has nothing to do with the subject at issue can be surprisingly fruitful. It is very desirable to foster such chance inputs.

Controlled or planned serendipity is one of the hidden motives behind the brainstorming principle – to generate as many ideas as possible. It is always surreptitiously hoped that one of the wild ideas will turn out quite by chance to be just what was wanted – even though, as Jantsch points out in his classic review of technological forecasting, the true value of brainstorming has never been proved. But the more prosaic purpose of these techniques is to place in front of the analyst a great variety of ideas which he will then examine to find the best.

There is certainly some virtue in holding an un-inhibited ideas meeting when nothing is too absurd to be suggested. I have not myself found these unstruc-tured methods very useful unless they are allied to techniques which generate a full list of alternatives systematically. The most important of these is known as the morphological approach, and was developed by Zwicky several years ago. Briefly, it consists of searching for solutions to a requirement by a form of discipline which forces the analyst to examine all combinations of all possible elements of his problem. The problem is first broken down into all the separate 'parameters' or elements, and then each element is given as many alternative values as can be imagined, thus forming a horizontal row. The totality of rows written down one under the other form a matrix known as a morphological chart; if one parameter value is picked from each row, then the resulting vertical chain is one complete solution from all the possible solutions. By studying all possible chains we have all possible solutions.

This technique in its original form is a prime plaything of a dedicated computer man, since it is tailormade for the automatic printing of vast numbers of chains. The first time I made a serious attempt to use it, the chart which we set up consisted of a matrix of about twenty rows with an average of about six alternatives in each row. So there was an astronomical number of solutions if we had bothered to generate them – around 10^{15} in fact. We did not generate them all. Unfortunately the problem was a military one which cannot be described here, but I can give the steps which were found useful in making the morphology manageable. The number of possible combinations was cut down by:

1. Intuitively excluding values which were at the extremes (i.e. clearly inferior to the existing value or wildly over-sophisticated).
2. Spending a great deal of time looking for the contradictory interrelationships, which prevent an alternative in one element if a particular one is chosen in another element.
3. Putting specifications or bounds on to any parameter where this was possible, and excluding any values outside this specification.
4. Ruthlessly ruling out any element of the problem which was not strictly fundamental to the primary problem objective (i.e. drawing the problem boundaries more tightly).
5. Discussing the broad range of solutions with the decision-maker to get a feel of how far he was prepared to move in any direction.

The result was that the number of solutions could be cut down until it was small enough for each to be looked at individually from cost and performance criteria, after which only a small spectrum of final preferred solutions emerged.

With hindsight, I felt that we might possibly have reached this same point by normal unstructured thinking without any greater difficulty, but this is impossible to verify. Certainly, the actual mainspring of the method – the generation of large numbers of solutions – was its weakest point. But there was no doubt that it had been a useful exercise, if only from the structure it introduced into the thinking, and the mere presence of the evolving morphological chart on the conference table helped to crystallise many discussions.

The structure which it gives is powerful on two counts. Firstly, because the elements into which the problem has to be broken down have to be chosen in such a way that they fit together without overlapping, if the chart is to make sense. This forces attention to be paid to the inherent differences between one element and another. Secondly, because after the chart has been formed, the alternatives can be left open-ended while new ideas or data come to light, and there is always a clear-cut place for these new thoughts to be inscribed.

The morphological method can be used at various stages of a project. For example, the chart shown in Fig. 5 was used as a structure for arguing out what was the best level of modelling the traffic for an event-based simulation of a particular cargo-handling operation.

On another occasion I used the morphological method to set down all the elements involved in the modulation and transmission of a signal in a communications system. This had striking payoff in showing a basic confusion which existed in the relative structural nature of modulation, multiplexing and quantifying which had been worrying me but which I had not been able to state clearly in an earlier attempt. The result was a much easier discussion at the next meeting of a group of experts.

Ship arrival description	Single periodic stream	Superimposition of several periodic streams	Single random deviate	Random deviate plus periodicity	Several random deviates
Method of generation	Historical pattern	re-synthesised from statistics of past traffic	a controlled pattern designed to test the system variables		
Fixed ship attributes	Constant	linked to specific ship arrivals	re-synthesised from past statistics		
Hatch pattern	Even over all hatches	Typical pattern	By 'commanding hatch' fraction of total		
Description of cargo	Ship homogeneous	Hold homogeneous	By 'batches'	By cargo class	By consignment

FIG. 5

Morphological research now comes in various guises, and in some it has perhaps been taken too seriously as making an original contribution – replacing brainstorming rather than assisting it. This is particularly tempting if the matrix is put into a computer. A technique of the sort is now being used by a market research team to generate possible trade names, for example. This is simply using the computer to do the routine work for which it is suited. But there has been some tendency to believe that generating the morphological solution chain is analogous to imagination: a French paper, for example, is in fact entitled 'Artificial Imagination'. This is false; the generation of combinations of elementary solution alternatives (even if bolstered with pre-set constraints on desirability weighting criteria) is of a quite different kind from the exercise of human imagination. It is as if a shopping-list were said to be equivalent to the mental picture of a full shopping-basket.

The morphological method originally devised by Zwicky was intended to be a specific technique – a method with its own procedure and rationale. But in application it tends to evaporate into an attitude of mind rather than a precise method. Its main success has been in technological innovation, but even here there is evidence that it is most useful as an aid to thought rather than a complete method in itself. Norris described how his use of it had developed after many tries, and my experience in more general fields of application confirms a view which he expresses that '. . . after drawing a morphological chart for a particular problem the chart should be thrown away and the design process continued independently', and '. . . the action of drawing up the morphological chart triggered off the mind into the right way of thinking as regards solving the problem'.

But it is going too far to recommend, as he does, that the technique should be developed until the procedure of eliminating unwanted solutions 'becomes more automatic and less dependent upon the intuition of the engineer'. That 'intuition' is in fact a vast assembly of experience and information, and until all this can be programmed for the morphological computer, which is unlikely in this century, the problem-solver's intuition is the best filter. The morphological computer's main role is to trigger ideas, not filter them.

The morphological attitude of mind may be the best way of avoiding the danger, after a great deal of brainstorming and 'depth thinking', of reaching conclusions which look brilliantly argued and comprehensive, only to find later that a vital possibility has been missed. This is particularly pertinent in pure think-tank work where possible futures are being imagined and their problems solved.

A worrying example of this occurred in the study of maximum security in prisons which I mentioned in the last chapter. The project team took the approach of making a conscious effort to think like an escapee and the escape organisers. Several interesting methods of escape were invented, the counters to them were worked out, and the cost-effectiveness of each method and its counter estimated. One of the more sophisticated – escape by a helicopter landing inside the prison perimeter while the prisoners were out of their cell-block – was found to be easily foiled by various simple devices which the prison staff could deploy, and this was therefore given a low probability of being used.

Three years later the helicopter method was actually used in the rescue of Joe Kaplan from a Mexican jail. It had many of the features dreamed up in the study: a helicopter rented several hundred miles away; the landing during a time when most prisoners and guards were in an entertainment period. But the team missed – inconceivably, with hindsight – the one feature which invalidates all the defensive counters of the prison staff, namely that *the helicopter was made to look official*. Painted in the blue and white colours of the Mexican Attorney-General's office, it was not attacked, it was saluted. And Kaplan got away. It was suspected that the whole thing was a C.I.A. operation, so the cost-effectiveness figures were rather distorted, but the principle should surely have been imagined.

What is the answer? In this case, deception methods had not been forgotten, but they had been linked only to *other* methods of escape, not to this particular one by helicopter. So in this case the answer – again with hindsight – was simple: insistence on a quick application of morphology even at a late stage, when all avenues had been deemed to have been explored. If all the constituent factors of all the different escape methods had been permuted, the Mexican plan would have emerged. This permutation to produce the complete set of all possibilities, however unlikely, is the basis of morphological research.

More generally, the group leader ought to be relentlessly suspicious of an apparently comprehensive list of solutions, and call frequently for fresh ideas. In this way the standard is kept at its peak and omissions are likely to be picked up. Better still, the group leader can dip into the project and bring a fresh mind to it in the hope that he will spot something the team has overlooked. In Chapter 4, I mentioned the 'pick-up' approach for use when things were going wrong. But to keep the standard of his group's work as high as possible, time should be found to pick up various elementary parts of each project, examine them in some detail, and put them down again – whether they are lagging behind or not. Leaving *all* the detailed thinking to the team is delegating too far and risking a gradually deteriorating standard. When the group leader is forced to delegate to this extent owing to his pressure of work, then the group has grown too far or too fast, as discussed in Chapter 2.

It seems generally agreed – for example, at a recent seminar on innovation – that creativity is most likely to be found in the smaller team, and the cell structure I suggested in Chapter 2 provides this basis. But it would be wrong to adopt all the conclusions of the enthusiasts and let the intellectual mixture get too heady. To assemble complete teams of 'wild ones' who would be kept out of day-to-day working, to spend their time continuously brainstorming and innovating, seems hardly justified even in a large organisation which may be able to afford them, since it is not going to make as fruitful a use of each innovation as putting together a mixture of innovators and non-innovators. And surely even the wild ones will produce better ideas if they have to follow their creativity by a little work in developing the idea, and have to get involved to some extent in the grass roots of the problem they are thinking about.

A further main issue in the search for effective thinking is the analyst's obligation to use the added power of modern tools of analysis wisely. These tools can handle larger problems but they bring with them awful dangers: principally that they can cause the truth to be obscured behind a smoke-screen of data.

The typical modern technique is a marriage between systematically applied mathematics and the use of a computer, the one feeding the other, and is genuinely powerful. For example, take the application of matrix algebra (of a far more complex kind than could be sensibly manipulated by hand; the computer plays a central role) to the problem of regional industrial planning. For each industry and service, a separate analysis is made of what resources it needs and what products it supplies. Then, when all the complex interactions between industries, services and transportation are stated, they can all be written down in matrix notation, and the whole 'input–output model' thrown at the computer. And solutions are obtained. But since the manipulation has gone on unseen, and because of the mass of data confronting him, the analyst may end up with a quantitative solution but no understanding.

No need to dwell here on the aphorisms that a computer output is only as accurate as its input data, and that the discipline which the computer imposes on the analyst is itself enough justification for using it. These truths have been pointed out often enough. The point is a little deeper than this. It concerns the fundamental tendency of professional men to head in the direction of complexity.

Simplicity has many virtues in problem-solving. The chief of these is that when the approach is simple there is a chance of grasping the whole of the problem in one intellectual span. The team then have a chance of embracing all aspects of it, and of looking with some human understanding at each relationship which their analysis is manipulating. When the approach is complex it can still be possible to think through the meaning behind any piece of mathematics, and to examine all the relationships which the model produces, but this takes an enormous amount of time. Many complex modern procedures can be fully grasped in this way only in a research environment, not a problem-solving environment where a solution is needed by a given deadline.

And since one of the prime sources of difficulty is the weakness of the assumptions which have to be made, it is wise to remember that the limitations of a simple assumption can be more easily understood and allowed for than those of a sophisticated assumption.

The conclusion from this is not that complexity should be abandoned (although sometimes this is certainly true), but that everyone concerned should have its dangers engraved on his heart. A model may have results sprouting from its surface, but if there is not the time to explore its interior, then the analyst is offering the decision-maker something which is based on an act of faith. He will be all right just so long as he keeps his fingers crossed.

The analyst can only uncross his fingers if he backs

up all such complex methods with a parallel, simpler approach. This is a fundamental rule and an essential discipline. It is not just insurance or faint-heartedness.

Another virtue of simplicity is that it often works just as well for much less effort. Sometimes the gain which complexity brings is quite illusory, since the detail (which is marginally worth having in a technical sense) can be more than offset by the problems which it gives administratively. An example of this was the reduction in detail of the passenger figures collected by railway station officials on the London commuting traffic. Statistics used to be based on actual passenger counts from each train, and the work involved (not to say the inaccuracies) was very heavy. Later it was decided to switch to broad descriptive categories only (full and standing, half full, quarter full, etc.). It was found that this provided all the accuracy needed for its purpose – the traffic forecasting and planning – and entailed of course very much less work. It also avoided introducing a lot of spurious accuracy.

On the other hand there is a hidden benefit from complexity which is seldom openly admitted since it is not very respectable. To get solutions adopted, it is often a fact of contemporary life that common-sense advice, or simple analyses which the decision-maker can understand (and could have done himself if he had been sufficiently systematically minded), may not carry the day unless it is supported by a computer-based analysis or something which looks equally sophisticated. If the analyst is sufficiently confident of the conclusions of the simple approach, but he knows that to get his conclusions adopted he must agree to carry out in parallel a complex approach which is suspect, then it takes an idealist to advise him not to. If the idealist's advice leads to a project with no concrete outcome, then it is bad advice; better advice is to live with the world as he finds it. Better still is to avoid getting himself into this position, and this must be a preoccupation of the group leader. If necessary he should refuse to take on a problem which is likely to have a commonsense answer if he knows that commonsense alone will not be enough, or a problem which he thinks can be solved simply if he knows the decision-maker only acts when blinded with science. There must be more useful ways of employing his group's talents.

Jargon comes in for much abuse, but one of the jargon phrases which has been in vogue deserves better. The phrase is 'conceptual thinking'. Quiet smiles sometimes appear when this is introduced into the conversation: jargon is often taken to be a smoke-screen for lack of precision. And indeed few people who use the phrase would find it easy to say what they mean by it.

A splendid interchange took place one afternoon in the Palais des Nations in Geneva. The transatlantic visitor was extolling the virtues of the 'management mode' in international assistance; what was needed was conceptual thinking. 'I'm glad you said that,' was the reply, 'because in the first three months of our new project we've done nothing but conceptual thinking.' 'Fine,' said the visitor, and settled back in his chair satisfied. Afterwards another official present said that the whole interchange had been meaningless to him.

But there was a serious meaning behind the jargon, as there usually is. In the early phase of a study, time should certainly be taken up thinking of new concepts; if the team can set up a new conceptual framework to work in, then their later work will bear their own stamp and will most likely be the better for it.

A striking example of a new conceptual framework was given in the two articles published by O. I. Franksen in 1969. He proposed a method aimed at giving economic analysis a greater depth of meaning by drawing the analogy with methods of analysis in the physical sciences. This is a most advanced piece of work which deserves a less esoteric audience. It shows precisely how an engineer, finding himself faced with a problem in economics, did not merely apply standard economic methods, but sat down and thought out at length a new framework on which his approach to modelling would be based. Who can doubt that the resulting analysis carried out by this author would be very much more effective by virtue of his conceptual thinking? But notice that his framework was of use only to analysts already trained in science or engineering. This is an interesting point: the conceptual framework can be intensely personal to the team; this is why it is important for a team to start by doing its own conceptual thinking rather than using someone else's.

Analogies can always be useful in the conceptual phase, and a trick, which is not as retrograde as it sounds, is to look at the problem from the point of view of an earlier era. I once gained a very useful insight into the basic concepts of the laying and sighting of artillery by going to a military library and reading how the gunners faced up to the problem in the last century. Again, the basic framework of integrated management of transport from door to door (the 'through transport' concept) is nicely illuminated by studying the earliest methods of trading. Several hundred years ago, through transport was often the normal mode, and it was the onset of modern trading patterns with their complexity and specialisation which gradually complicated and fragmented the framework. This earlier situation clearly repays a little study if we are finding now that the trend is being reversed.

A useful framework for analysis is to adopt the stage-by-stage approach which is the basis of optimisation via dynamic programming. This involves breaking down the problem into a series of sub-problems; dynamic programming has shown the usefulness of solving the last one first and working backwards along the route of the best solution. This type of approach can be applied more widely, even when optimisation is not the aim.

Another example of conceptual thinking was in the team who began to notice a resemblance between the flows of products between different sectors of industry as set out in an input–output matrix of the type mentioned earlier, and the flows of goods between origin and destination in a transportation model. This was a purely artificial concept but it led to a way of ordering the various industries and services which allowed the analyst to get a better grasp of their interdependence, and to visualise the relationships buried in the matrix instead of merely manipulating rows of figures.

In summary, conceptual thinking means, before getting down to the methods of analysis themselves, taking the problem to pieces, getting a feel for its structure, and considering how to set out a systematic framework in which solutions can be discussed. Of course, it cannot all be done at once (the 'three months doing nothing but conceptual thinking' was said with the tongue in the cheek); and a certain amount of the analysis has to go hand in hand with the concept-building. But the project should never be started without spending a little time in such thinking before diving into the detail.

Much of the conceptual thinking will be triggered off at brainstorming meetings, which many writers see only as a fruitful source of new ideas. I see them as playing a fuller and more closely integrated part in the team's work.

Earlier in this chapter I mentioned Jantsch's conclusion on brainstorming. After reviewing the way in which a number of organisations had gone about brainstorming meetings, he pointed out that in spite of all the enthusiasm there was little hard evidence of success. In my view this could well be because of the narrow role which brainstorming is normally given. Jantsch reviews several approaches, and it is interesting that they are mainly confined to cross-fertilisation meetings between staff from a number of different branches, and to meetings which take place before and after the normal analytical work of the project team. Once again, this is the alternation between vertical and lateral thinking, but it seems to place the emphasis a bit askew. It is vital to avoid looking on the analysts as the vertical thinkers and the outsiders as adding the lateral element. If this is encouraged, then the project team can become too formal and sterile in their approach. It is the team themselves who should be assembled for brainstorming, with or without outsiders, and such meetings can be allowed to slip gracefully into a normal technical discussion. By using devices such as a morphological chart, and by keeping them in front of the team during the brainstorming meetings, the thinking can shift imperceptibly between vertical and lateral and take on the strengths of each.

*

There are other marks of a good team than innovative thinking and conceptual thinking. One of these is the determination to dig deep.

It needs persistence if the standard of work is to be kept high, for example by repeatedly reopening and reconsidering in depth problems which it would be tempting to say were already adequately solved. The impatient may reject the idea of spending several hours discussing a point over again. We saw in the previous chapter that if no notes are taken at the first discussion, the second one may waste time going over precisely the same ground. Given the notes, however, it is often possible either to dig deeper than last time or to have a fresh insight. In fact, the mere existence of a break and a resumption may bring a new idea, as when taking up a crossword puzzle a second time and quickly finding clues that were elusive the day before under the most intense thought.

The theory of human problem-solving developed by Newell and Simon explains this as the build-up of a short-term store of working knowledge about the way the problem has been tackled so far, which cannot consciously be erased and so encumbers the solving process. After the break this store has partly emptied and the analyst can go back to his earlier state of knowledge and move quickly again in a new direction. (The part which is not emptied goes over into the longer-term memory and forms the learning process.)

Persistence in depth of thinking has to be matched by persistence in pursuing the approach adopted past all obstacles. Sometimes analyses are abandoned for sheer lack of energy, sapped more often than not by the analysts' dawning awareness of the deficiencies of their methods. Some of these deficiencies are described in the next chapter; they may be inevitable and may have to be accepted if the problem is not to be abandoned as insoluble.

The main weakness of analysis which the problem-solver has to learn to live with is repeatedly having to make concessions to reality and accuracy. His whole approach has to be a balance between skimming over the surface and drowning in the depths (walking on the water with measured tread is extremely difficult). He knows, or should know, more like a politician than an engineer, that he can never fully solve anything. This means that he has to be very strong in spirit.

Another problem which the less confident analyst will run into, and on which he needs reassurance, is that sometimes the results of using a quite advanced and difficult technique are, with hindsight, intuitive. They may be conclusions which could have been reached either by qualitative reasoning or by a much simpler quantitative method. But what do we mean by 'could have been'? That fact is that they weren't, and it may genuinely have been necessary to do the advanced work. The outsider finds it only too easy to smile at the naïvety until he is asked to explain why he had never reached that conclusion himself. The analyst may be quite unable to recall whether or not he himself knew the conclusion before he started, and may be tempted – pessimistically – to believe he has achieved nothing when in fact he has produced a brand-new conclusion.

This point is discussed by McCall in the context of the contribution of probabilistic methods to classical economics. He makes the interesting point that some of the antagonisms which have sprung up in this field are due to the fact that, after they have been explained, many of the results which could only have been achieved with stochastic models can then be rationalised as 'intuitive'.

I remember a case where, using a simple deterministic model in parallel with a stochastic model, the main additional conclusion which the latter model brought – after consuming a much bigger slice of the resources – was that although it could not be reliably quantified, there was so much system flexibility that the results of the simple model were true only under conditions of fixed-cost operations. There were many ways in which the system could be made to do better according to the main performance criteria, but always at increased cost. Again, this seemed intuitively obvious when explained, but would not have been brought out without the complex model.

One of the main problems is the lack of sufficiently good data. The analyst may try his best to get it, but what if he cannot? Dare he guess? The scientific answer is no. Information theory will point out that guesswork destroys information, and statistical theory will show how the unsupported data cannot be of value. The trouble is that both these views contradict commonsense. Guesswork at the core of a problem is not reasonable, certainly, but guesswork based on commonsense views at the fringe of a problem is surely sometimes justified.

For example, there will always be relationships which crop up in a study which are known to be increasing in a certain direction, but whose form is not known and cannot be measured. Is the analyst to assume no relationship, or to make a crude estimate and use it? The danger of any guess is that it is most probably wrong, but the danger of no guess is that the resulting behaviour will not only be wrong but will also be too simple. The loss of a possible dimension of complexity can sometimes be a sufficient reason for putting in something, believing that the guess is less dangerous than the no-guess. (I am assuming that the usual precaution of a sensitivity test has shown that the guess is important.)

If such estimates or guesses *are* put into a model, there is a danger that they are lost within it and after a time their existence is forgotten. People using the model then come to have a false confidence in its reliability. To present this it is vital to keep the guess-work parameters well to the forefront as an explicit part of the data input, so that their values always have to be reconsidered before the model can be manipulated.

Such guesswork is no doubt easier in mechanistic relationships than in human ones. In a mathematical model of radar reflections from anomalous terrain, to study the dangers of radar altimeters, some law had to be assumed governing the density of moisture content of a tree, viewed from above, as the foliage increased. Clearly, the top of a tree is less dense than its middle, but on the average what is the law: linear? highly exponential? By assuming a reasonable exponential form based on common sense, the model could be completed, and the results were later confirmed by experiment as being reasonably correct.

In less mechanistic matters the dangers of confusing common sense with personal prejudice are much greater. In the debate over the value to Britain of joining the Common Market, the following remark was made after the complaint that the Government White Paper did not give a figure for the effect of entry on the balance of payments:

This is unquantifiable. You cannot be lured by a false statistical exactitude into abandoning your common sense. My personal opinion is that on a common sense judgement the prizes of entry will outweigh the costs. Some other people would like to put it all through a computer, but I don't think the computer has yet been invented which could do this job.

This displays an underlying caution about the mystique of a computer which is very welcome. But one might well argue that the speaker has loaded the term 'common sense' with the meaning that his own judgement is the natural judgement of the world at large (the basic meaning of 'common sense'). Where, as here, a contrary opinion exists, then common sense is not common sense at all. (I cannot resist the temptation of recalling the two letters in *The Times*, side by side, giving the directly opposite views on this point, each signed by their protagonists among professional economists. I believe the score was something like 42 for and 46 against.) But when all those concerned agree that common sense dictates a relationship or a piece of data as being roughly in a certain area, and it is not possible to measure it, then an estimate – albeit a conservative one – may be admitted. The analyst should appreciate that in the real world there is a partial truth in the old aphorism that the improbable is less likely than the impossible, with its splendid illustration of the improbable being that the Prime Minister will slap the Queen on the back and offer her a cigar.

And the pursuit of accuracy can be very wasteful of valuable thinking time. In spite of the law of diminishing returns in pursuing the accuracy of analysis, there is a type of intellectual laziness which may lead an analyst to go deeper than he should. It is much more relaxing to work through the mathematics and manipulate quantitative data, with its comforting overtones of certainty and routine, than to enter the muddy waters of the qualitative aspects and grapple with conflicting subjective judgements. The group leader will normally be well advised to steer teams slightly towards the qualitative, to neutralise the tendency in the opposite direction.

'Follow not the truth too near the heels lest it dash out thy teeth' is a fashionable proverb to quote this year. Perhaps it should be modified to '. . . lest thou hast no breath left to question him when thou arrivest at his house'.

6 Dangerous Thinking

'Alors s'édifient les constructions..., rationelles en apparence, absurdes parce que le point de départ est faux, mais mortellement dangereux pour leurs victimes parce que personne... ne prend la peine de revenir au point de départ et de vérifier les faits.'
André Maurois, *Les Nouveaux Discours du Dr O'Grady*

When in the last chapter ways of encouraging more creative thinking were discussed, it was tacitly assumed that the project team were at least fully competent in the skills of their profession. But competence has two aspects: sheer technical skills, which can be taught, and understanding, which often cannot. Applying an advanced technique of analysis without sufficient depth of understanding is doubly dangerous; it not only may produce the wrong answers, but may encourage everyone concerned – including the analyst – to believe that with such a powerful tool the answers must be right.

Even if one cannot teach experience, what can be done is to point out the main dangers which may face the team, in the hope that they may be recognised in time and headed off. This is the aim of this chapter.

Although the outcome of a project may satisfy its written objectives, and may be all that the decision-maker desired, it is often based on assumptions and approximations which the analyst himself felt were less than acceptable. Such partial failure, when it is clearly known to the analyst himself, may not be unhealthy; it may be the very best that could be done, and often better than giving the decision-maker no guidance at all. The state of the art has to be advanced, and to do so it has to strain to tackle problems for which it is barely equipped, getting close enough to the truth to justify the attempt.

But if the failure is not recognised by the analysts; if they wrongly believe in their unsound conclusions; if they see accuracy where there is none; if they believe they have found the best solution when they have not; then there is going to be trouble. Very regrettably, teams can get away with work of this sort long enough for the natural forces that shift them to new pastures to come into play before their unsound work backfires. They may never have it brought home to them that anything is wrong, and so they can continue to believe in themselves.

What are these areas of self-deception? I would rank the following as being the five most pervasive:

1. Believing that a mathematical model represents reality.
2. Believing that the future can be forecast.
3. Believing that an optimum value is the right solution.
4. Believing that all criteria of goodness can be measured and combined.
5. Believing that if it is done by computer it must be better.

The use of models in problem-solving has been implicit in the previous chapters. The types of model with which our problem-solving group will be most concerned are mathematical, and it is here that most of the dangers lie, since there seems to be a feeling that a mathematical model is something quite different from all other types. Pritsker and Kiviat classify models as symbolic models (flow diagrams and computer programs), iconic models (scale models, maps, globes) and analogue models (electrical circuits, hydraulic and mechanical devices). I would also add as a class conceptual models such as the diagrams which tend to be generated during the conceptual phase described in the last chapter; these are in the same class as the artist's image or poet's dream mentioned by the same authors.

No one would believe that the latter classes of model represent real life in any concrete sense, but mathematical and logical models have an air about them which can lead to a delusion among analysts building and using them. This is that the relationships which emerge from model manipulation are true – or at least true enough as not to need further examination. (This is particulary noticable when the symbolic models are assembled with connecting logic into a computer-based simulation model which is then used to carry out 'experiments'.) Again, to quote Pritsker and Kiviat, 'the best that can be said for a model is that it does its job'.

One trouble is that inexperienced analysts may be mistaken in just what *is* the job of a model. If it is an architect's model of a building then its primary role is fairly clear: it helps him to visualise the design and allows him to pass on his concepts to others. This is a very limited role. There is little intention that the scale model will tell him anything about the way the building will function. But just as the architect's model is worth building merely to assist visualisation, so sometimes is a symbolic model.

In the case of an analogue model (a small working model of a machine, say, or an aerodynamic model for wind-tunnel tests), the second role is the main one; it is hoped that an insight will be gained into the behaviour of the real thing. But no one would go from such a working model direct to the final design without first confirming the behaviour with a full-size prototype. How is it, then, that when we come to the symbolic model, the next step after studying model behaviour is often to present the results to the decision-maker as if they were true and could at once be transferred to real life without any prototype stage?

The reason for this licence, the reader may object, is that when we are faced with social, economic or organisational problems (for that matter, all except the purely mechanistic), there is just no possibility of building a prototype. True, but if so how much more should we then mistrust the results which emerge from symbolic models. And how very dangerous are the teams who are prepared to make recommendations on the basis of hasty last-minute manipulations of a mathematical model which took rather longer to build than had been expected.

In fact, if we went to the relevant scientific discipline of semiotics (the use of signs to represent reality), we might be even more pessimistic. Colin Cherry discussed the danger of believing that there is any validity at all in the description of situations and organisations in symbolic and mathematical form. In particular, he points to the danger of transferring models which hold well enough at one point to another point. In physics the concepts of space and time can be safely assumed to be universal, wheras in sociology space and time mean geography and history. 'We cannot take a model of some social phenomenon and transfer it to another epoch, or another part of the world.' This may seem obvious when written down, but it is a point which very often slips past without being considered by an analyst.

It is particularly dangerous when a team uses a

standard approach, with a particular structure developed for one problem, to solve a different problem merely by changing parameter values. Even if they make some structural changes, there is still danger. One example of this is the team which fails to notice the degree of sophistication of the environment in which they are working and applies advanced techniques because they 'are educated beyond realising how backward the state of affairs really is'. In the extreme, such specialists may be found tackling a problem which does not exist because the world is not as they imagined it to be and exists only in their model.

A project leader may often be faced with the choice between adapting a model which was built for a different purpose or building a new one. The arguments for adaptation are usually economic, and often they are genuine. It should be realised, however, that a special danger exists when such existing models are massaged into a new shape. This is that the fresh approach, tailored precisely to the new problem environment, will be inhibited; there is bound to be some degree of compromise between what is done and what would have been done if a new model had been built from scratch. This may be easily argued away by rationalising the act: 'I would have done it this way anyhow.' Most likely this is not true – a little more self-delusion. A fresher team would probably have made a different departure. And strongest of all is the danger that, hidden in the old model, were assumptions – buried deep because they were implicit – which do not in fact apply to the later application, but are never questioned.

Some workers see the inaccuracies of their models merely as imposed by the constraints of their computer – available storage capacity and speed. Then (another aspect of Parkinson's Law) they consider that the best solutions will result from using the fullest capacity of computer resources. There is then a choice: either to get exact solutions to a simple model, or to get approximate solutions to a detailed model. The wise will proceed by tackling problems from both directions, and the wiser still will also co-ordinate the work of the model with what Kornai terms 'heuristic, intuitive and improvised human intellectual activity'. This co-ordination is to be at every stage: 'in the construction of the model and in the partly subjective estimation of the data; during the computation, in determining the computation series and sensitivity tests to be carried out; and finally, in the evaluation and analysis of the results and in actual decision-making'.

All this is extremely sound and expresses well how arid by comparison is a routine mechanical application of a model. But even analysts who would agree with such sentiments may still regard their modelling activity as the fundamental element in the work and other intellectual activity as ancillary to it. It is this view which needs to be questioned. In the great majority of projects the boot is, or should be, on the other foot; the model should be put in its place as merely a tool to assist in the intellectual activity. When put in this rightful place it is surprising how a project plan looks unbalanced and needs to be restyled, with more time and effort spent thinking and less spent calculating.

Scoffing at models is, I suppose, an old sport, based always on the twin criticisms of inaccurate data and unjustified assumptions. Just occasionally the authors of a report are quite candid, as in that of a United Nations Working Group: 'The number of assumptions which could be made is limitless.' I would suggest that, viewed honestly and in cold blood, this is nearly always the case. It is a nice piece of self-deception to see only a set range of assumptions – assumption 1, assumption 2, assumption 3, all neatly labelled – when most probably an imaginative critic could think of a stream of new assumptions which would have an equal claim to be examined.

Of course, to make any progress at all with the model the range of alternative assumptions has to be confined at some point. Generally, tests of sensitivity are used to weed out assumptions which do not make much difference anyway, but this is rarely a clear-cut device. Trouble with assumptions was partly the cause of what must surely be the bitterest modelling controversy of recent times: the World Model of the Club of Rome project on 'The Predicament of Mankind', as reported in *Limits to Growth*.

This controversy is worth considering because much of it has been about the accuracy of modelling, not about the world environment. Typical of the comments which *Limits to Growth* gave rise to are these two, taken from different issues of the same journal:

'. . . likely to be one of the most important documents of our age'.
'. . . an empty and misleading work'.

The first of these two extremes expresses, perhaps, the uncritical view of a layman who was impressed with the conclusions of the work as a whole, and the second the highly critical view of professionals who were obsessed with the techniques employed. As such we can understand the difference. But what are we to think of the comment by these same professionals that the report 'pretends to a degree of certainty so exaggerated as to obscure the few modest (and unoriginal) insights. . .', and in similar vein in an eminently respectable and well-argued general survey of the environmental problem: '*The Limits to Growth* [which] predicts that industrial society will collapse half-way through the twenty-first century.' Because this is in fact precisely what the project did not do – predict. And it certainly did not pretend to any certainty at all, let alone an exaggerated one, as any who had read carefully the introduction and final commentary will have seen. For example, the central conclusion of the project is given in these words (p. 23): 'If the present growth trends in world population, industrialisation, pollution, food production, and resources depletion continue unchanged, the limits to growth on this planet will be reached sometime within the next one hundred years.' I hope the reader will pause and wonder at such a degree of misunderstanding.

I believe the reason is that the critics concentrated on the *model* itself and not on the intellectual arguments which went with it. This is clearly the wrong emphasis. The objective of the project was to study the relationships involved, not to carry out any predictions. This was stated by the authors, and rightly so since this is what models should be used for.

But the authors themselves are not completely innocent of false emphasis. While it is clear to the objective reader of *Limits to Growth* that the modelling itself was supported by a great deal of thoughtful intellectual activity, the authors still placed the emphasis on the model, its newness, and the originality of the emergent results – however much they qualify them – instead of using it simply as an ancillary tool to their excellent arguments. The relationships which they put forward as model discoveries – modes of behaviour, possibilities of a runaway or collapse – are in fact derivable analytically; they are built-in mathematical modes which are nothing new, as the critics point out virulently. The professional reader has been offended by this wrong emphasis and blinded to the fact that the sensitivities and detailed interactions between many of the input hypotheses of world behaviour are not analytically predictable. It is these which add great strength to the project rationale and certainly prevent the report from being 'empty and misleading'.

Why did the authors feel impelled to put the emphasis thus on the model results (for example by placing the original computer print-out in front of the reader) to an extent that the community at large sees only sophisticated computer prediction? Probably because the world at large (the main audience, since this report was written to have a wide impact) has at the moment a kind of admiration, mixed with hate, for computer-based work, and it is effective to use such admiration to gain acceptance which would not otherwise have been accorded. If the computer-based model had been put in its rightful place as an instigator of thought about structure, and as a stickler for accurate input data – its results being only rough numerical indicators of relationships that could be argued out in words – would the unprofessional reader have been so impressed? Almost certainly not. Hence, on a corollary to my Chapter 1 dogma that a solution which is not implemented is a poor solution, the authors took the right course.

More generally, what should the analyst do about

this computer mystique which the outside world imposes on his work? Should he use it to gain his audience's attention and interest? This is a matter for the individual. What is certain is that, whether he uses it or fights it, the analyst must at least be conscious of what he is doing.

The other and more penetrating criticisms of the Club of Rome report hark back to the other main weakness of models – the variety of assumptions used. For example, several different assumptions are put in about the control mechanisms of technological advance, and the effect on world stability is calculated for each. But, just as in the United Nations report quoted, the number of assumptions is really almost limitless, and critics may point to many more things that could happen to change the picture. For example, the effect of gradual deterioration taking place at different speeds according to local differences in environment and social conditions could be assumed to have a strong impact on the reaction of the rest of the world where things are deteriorating more slowly. The sad thing is that the vehemence of the methodological discussion is such that it prevents the discussion of substance from having a proper airing.

When an analyst constructs a model to help him solve a problem, he needs some assurance that it represents enough of the real world, at a good enough level of accuracy, to make the exercise worth while. But how is he to go about getting this? If it is the future he is studying (and it normally is), and if he will be wanting to try out changes in the problem system (which again he normally will), then how is he to approach the question of testing the model? The future does not exist to be tested against, and the system is to be changed so that present accuracy does not necessarily imply future accuracy. He will have a methodological problem on his hand as well as the original problem.

There is no solution to this. A model can be made self-consistent – true to itself – and this itself is important since there is then a systematic aid to thought. It will allow intuitive relationships to be explored more widely for their own sake, not pretending that they are real-world relationships, but hoping that the exploration will give an insight into the relationships which do exist.

Sometimes it is possible to go further and calibrate a model against present data, to the extent that over a reasonable range of variation its behaviour agrees with the history of what happened in the real system. This is often termed 'validation', but of course it is proving validity in a very limited sense. It says little or nothing about the validity of the model as a tool for studying possible changes in the problem system which have not yet been tried. It is only in retrospect that we can be sure that a model was valid, when the solution has been introduced and the predicted model behaviour is found to occur in reality. And that is rather late for most of us. It is wise to avoid using the word 'validation' for the test of a predictive model against past behaviour.

This final degree of confidence can only be achieved in advance on closely defined and fully mechanistic systems (and even here it is worth bearing in mind that in many cases a physical mock-up can be cheaper). There is a limited range of problems, such as those in electronic signal processing, where a mathematical model can – without incurring very heavy costs – be made fully reliable in predicting the behaviour of a new system. But in general this will not be so. More often, all that the analyst can do, on the basis of his past experience and of analogous work on different applications, is to make a well-judged act of faith that the model behaviour will illumine the problem truly and not falsely.

The act of faith is made easier if the more doubtful model is placed in a hierarchical relationship with another model in which more confidence can be placed. For example, an interesting but doubtfully realistic war-game can be made to produce enough points of performance to set up an analytical model; this can be used to explore relationships over a wider range which includes situations which actually occurred in field exercises; and the exercises themselves may be considered to have adequate similarity to real warfare. (A tortuous chain, but one which has been used successfully.) Less esoteric, perhaps, was a study of the impact of modern technology on a lighthouse service. Here interacting models were used in three levels: a first level to analyse general policies of transport modes, of centralisation, of the use of helicopters, etc., over the whole service; a second level to study more detailed operating patterns to decide how many vehicles would be needed to cover a particular region once a particular policy had been adopted; and a third level to study how to get better performance in maintenance schedules and manning reliefs once a particular allocation of vehicles had been made.

In developing such a hierarchy, there is a danger that at each level a good case can be made for quite a broad overlap with the neighbouring model. (In fact a purist will point out that it is impossible to do any of the levels properly without doing them all at once.) There will be pressure to build one large total system model at the same level of detail. But this type of model is the most dangerous of all since its inner workings are the most mysterious. When a hierarchical approach is decided on during a wise and realistic period of conceptual thinking, it must never be allowed to coalesce into a single organic whole when the team are buried in the detailed work; they will be thinking a good deal less wisely at that stage. Each level will have its own objectives, inputs and outputs, which of course must as far as possible fit in with each other. But if they do not fit exactly it will most often be better to live with a blurring of the edges than to try to force the joint.

Usually the tendency should be in the other direction – to disaggregate the component parts of a model and analyse the behaviour of each separately, so that such behaviour can be intuitively understood. This will be at the risk of losing some interactions between the sub-models, of course, but this is often the lesser danger. For example, in a multi-dimensional analysis of a number of commodity flows it may be better for understanding if each commodity is studied one at a time in all aspects, plus where necessary looking at all commodities together in one aspect, rather than building a single model which handles all commodities from all aspects. There will be some repetition in this, but of the type which reinforces rather than merely duplicates.

One of the temptations for analysts who are not closely controlled is to make simplifying mathematical assumptions which are plausible at a quick glance (and a quick glance is sometimes all that they ever get from anyone but their originator), but which can be sufficiently wide of the truth as completely to invalidate the mathematical results. For example, queueing models which work only for uncorrelated arrival and service time statistics may encourage the junior to assume that there *is* no correlation, for otherwise the approach may be impossible. But if correlation does exist then he is wasting his time; the results may not merely be inaccurate, they may be totally irrelevant to real-life behaviour. Whoever saw an infinite queue?

Because it is so difficult to achieve model behaviour which is close to real-world behaviour, I must re-emphasise a point made in an earlier chapter. As the results start to emerge (not after all the work is finished), they must be discussed with a practical man who knows about real life. I guarantee that the team will have to do some re-checking and re-running of the model after they have left him. Perhaps the last word on this subject should go to Bertrand Russell. After his intensive search with Whitehead for a logical basis for the axioms of mathematics, he wrote:

> In the end it seemed to result that none of the raw material of the world has smooth logical properties, but that whatever appears to have such properties is constructed artificially in order to have them.

So much has already been written about the dangers of forecasting that I would have liked to believe that every analyst had as deep an appreciation of them as can be written down here. Certainly, in discussion most people appear to agree that 'the only thing you can be sure of about a forecast is that it will be wrong'. But in spite of this there continues to be a good deal of mistaken forecasting going on, and I wonder whether there is a form of natural self-deception at play here too, fed by the desperate need to get some forecast at all costs if any progress is to be made. It has only recently become respectable to admit that (except for very limited cases) fore-telling the future course of events is impossible.

The philosophy of this subject is discussed fully in a recent P.E.P. report by de Hoghton, Page and Streatfield. The content of the work is the so-called new art of futurology rather than the old-fashioned quasi-science of forecasting, and this is in itself significant. The difference between them is largely a change of emphasis: for example, a more imaginative attempt is made to think of future events which will determine the trends, rather than to look at the trends themselves.

There are some areas where forecasting is reasonably safe. There is very little uncertainty, for example, in some short-term macro-economic forecasts in a stable national environment, since the momentum (and by the same token the inertia) of the economy is such a monolithic beast. It may be very difficult to control, but at least it is fairly certain that over a year or so there will be only a small percentage change in the level of production or of unemployment. At a different level it is reasonable to predict with some confidence the growth of general cargo imports through a seaport, since these are made up of the sum of numerous commodities each with its own trend, but dangerous to try to predict the future of one major bulk commodity which can in one blow be affected by a single event. In less stable societies and situations where cataclysmic events do tend to happen, and in all cases where we want to predict well ahead, we should not be surprised by major changes of a size which if predicted would have had scorn poured on them.

The emphasis, then, is on events, not on trends.

How little reliance can be placed on trends is illustrated by Moroney in a sad tale of sales forecasting. He shows how a clear upward trend indicating a boom in sales can in fact be due to the inertia of sales caused by a previous event (a change in the market) which had already taken place and then been reversed before the forecasting exercise was started. All trend analysis at that time, however sophisticated, pointed purely and simply in the wrong direction, and a much better estimate of future sales could have been got by taking the sales manager's intuitive opinion.

Hidden and delayed effects on trends are plentiful and, taken together with the fair probability of a cataclysmic event, make trend extrapolation so doubtful that it is often absurd to do any form of time-series analysis and projection forward. Laying a rule along the trend line by eye is as likely as not to give as close an answer to the future truth as any detailed analysis, however much comfort the latter may give.

Of course, many forecasting problems are impossible to solve with a ruler, since they are multi-dimensional and involve the combination of a number of correlated variables each based on incomplete data. In such cases the sophisticated method may be the only one; but it will still be equally likely to be proved quite wrong in the face of the unexpected.

Gross errors of forecasting are not limited to trend extrapolation or even to quantitative matters in general. An example of laughably mistaken qualitative predictions is the phenomenon of the wise men who time and again have stated that all there is to be known is already known. In the nineteenth century this was said several times, and even now in specialised fields it still crops up, in spite of all the contrary evidence that there is no limit to the depth of understanding of any subject. For example, Menne was prepared to say in 1962 that as a result of applying modern logical calculus to the classical syllogism, definitive answers have been obtained, and 'reasearch at this point even appears to have been concluded'. One can hardly imagine a more closely confined area of study, but even so I myself confidently predict that his statement will cause amusement to future logicians. What we witness in such cases is not bad forecasting so much as unwillingness to believe in a changed future.

One of the reasons why self-deception can flourish among forecasters is that more often than not the chickens are not given the time to come home to roost. By the time the forecast is proved wrong the forecaster has often moved on to fresh pastures, but even when he has not he finds it very easy to explain away his mistakes – even to himself. De Bono points out that prophets of doom are never shaken in their faith when the day of doom passes without incident. Their faith always manages to provide them with a rational let-out. In the same way, forecasters who are proved wrong can always find a critical change in the system they were talking about to account for their errors: their faith in the *method* may be quite unshaken. But if the method was of a kind which was likely to collapse in the face of a change, then it is the method itself which must be criticised.

It has been traditional with many decision-makers to ask for a single best forecast of the expected future situation, and for a small range of alternative investment proposals so that he can judge which to choose. The change is now towards providing the decision-maker with a range of forecasts any one of which may come true, and a range of investment proposals showing how each one matches up to each future situation. The choice will now be a genuine one of risk-judgement by the man who will have to be responsible for it, and in an uncertain situation the right choice may be the proposal which is the most robust to anything which may happen. Operational research tools such as a 'payoff matrix' may be added to give better estimation of the risks, but there is still a strong swing back to the role of the decision-maker himself.

If the analyst encounters, as I have, a decision-maker who asks for a single forecast and relies entirely on the analyst as to how it is arrived at (a throw-back to the analysts he is used to, who blinded him with forecasts derived from regression lines and exponential smoothing. . .), then it seems rather weak and apologetic to have to say: 'Look, I can't tell you the future. I can only point out a whole range of things which could happen.' But it must be done, and it ought to be possible to bring home to him the fact that this is a much healthier state of affairs. It is transferring back to the man who knows the business the task of judging what may or may not happen, as well as what policy is the more appropriate if it does happen. There is still plenty of work for the analyst in arriving at a realistic set of possible futures.

For longer-term forecasts – genuine futurology – the P.E.P. report goes even further. It is suggested that 'the role of the student of the future is not a prophet but a look-out'. The analyst not only has to think out what might be the alternative futures and what effect they will have on policy, but he has to advise the decision-maker on what to look for to see which one is approaching. He has to set up a simple set of parameters which can be monitored, to show what is happening as it happens – early enough for the policy to be adjusted accordingly. The forecaster has to become the man who says what direction to look in and what to watch for. If he has done this he can move on to his fresh pastures with a clear conscience.

Forecasting is bound up with the interpretation of correlations between variables, and here, in spite of all the standard teaching of every course in statistics, nothing seems to stop people from drawing conclusions from correlations which may be quite spurious. At the time of writing, the financial press is discussing the 'new' correlation which has been discovered between British stock market prices and the money supply. As one commentator points out – yet again:

> The existence of a correlation between these two variables does not by itself prove that the relationship works one way or the other. Moreover, the existence of an historical relationship is no guide to the future; conditions change and so does the behaviour of an economy. Unfortunately there seems to be a serious danger in the City of investors overlooking these factors and simply taking a slavish view of the effects of changes in the money supply.

Clearly, the analysts here are failing to get the message about the future through to their principals, even if they see the dangers themselves. There is a desperate need, it seems, to latch on to something new in the hope that it will do better than the old. But unless it is done with extreme circumspection, that is most unlikely.

*

The third form of dangerous thinking which I listed was the belief that an optimum value is the right solution. Even if a model is a pale shadow of reality, it may be felt that, whatever its shortcomings, the optimum value which it produces is what we should go for.

It does seem plausible, at first sight, to say that once it has been decided that a particular mathematical model is the best that can be built, then the optimum value which it points to is the solution which ought to be put forward. But this is not so, for several reasons, not least of which is the analyst's old bugbear – the choice of optimisation criteria. However, let us put this aside for a moment and assume that the analyst is at least working to the right criteria.

There is a substantial body of technique devoted to location of the optimum value of a multi-dimensional function – finding the highest point of a multidimensional surface. Such techniques can be extremely effective in minimising the amount of searching that has to be done to find this point, but the fact that they do such minimising means of course that there will be points left unexplored. Exploring every combination of parameter values is much looked down on by optimisation specialists as a method of brute force. Be that as it may, when it can be done without too much waste of effort and computer time then there is a good case for it, because whatever the efficiency of the optimisation algorithm, by definition it has a small probability of homing into a local optimum rather than the global optimum; and when one's competitor is found later to be doing rather better than oneself, it is little consolation to know that it was most unlucky that this very small chance actually occurred.

Even more fateful, and more likely, is the chance of glossing over an Achilles' heel – a hole in the more complex surface which would have been formed by adding one more factor to the model. And since there usually are several such extra factors, this should be a real worry to an analyst who is relying solely on an automatic search for the optimum. A good answer is to find a number of likely solutions and spread them out in front of a joint session of the project team and the decision-maker, for them to be picked to pieces under the arc-lamp of experience and of imagination about the future and what may go wrong. If there has been an earlier decision to exclude a particular factor from the model, then it must be brought back into the discussion at this stage to be considered qualitatively.

Indeed, I would put it forward as fundamental to the overwhelming majority of such analyses that the final selection of alternative solutions must be manual. Better still, and closely related to the lateral – vertical – lateral rhythm discussed in the previous chapter, is to alternate optimisation stages and manual selection stages so as to get a progressive climb to a reasoned, robust and at the same time mathematically favourable solution. The exceptions to this rule are those classical problems – such as transport scheduling – where automatic optimisation may produce such a clear-cut payoff that a simple-minded acceptance of the mathematical solution may be justified.

But what about the criteria by which to judge such solutions? On the rare occasion when there is one single criterion, there is only the danger of having chosen wrongly. But when there are several criteria, there is another danger: believing that all criteria of goodness can be measured and combined.

There are criteria – for example, the cruise passengers' preference for colourful chaos on arrival in port mentioned in Chapter 1 – which it would be absurd to try to quantify. Attempts will always be made: how much extra would the passengers pay for this local colour? How many passengers would be put off booking again by the uninteresting modern terminal? Equally qualitative and subjective are several of the factors by which the desirability of major development projects are judged these days: for example, the effect of the choice of site upon the environment. And here there really has been a determined attempt to put numbers to qualitative criteria.

Take the question of airport noise. One thinks immediately of the work done for the Roskill Commission's report on the siting of the Third London Airport. A very thorough attempt was made 'to put a cash figure on the nuisance that would be caused to residents near each site by airport noise, so that this "intangible" effect could be given its proper importance in relation to the other costs and benefits involved'. The course which had to be adopted nicely illustrates the fundamental problem. For instance, although the survey was quite properly heavily disguised so that emotional responses over the subject of the inquiry were ruled out, there was a substantial number of people who, faced with a hypothetical house near the airport, would not live in it at any price, and who also said that no amount of compensation could induce them to move from their present home. This can only be taken to imply that the nuisance value of the airport to them in their existing home would be infinite, and this was freely admitted by the team. But since the methodology would not tolerate infinite values, this portion of the distribution of values had to be truncated. And in choosing the truncation figure, the analyst's own value-judgement was intruding itself, thereby begging the question. In general, if when trying to put a cash value on a qualitative factor the answer comes out at infinity, then the wise course is to stop and try a different approach. The existence of the infinite value gives the lie to the attempt.

Another example was in the planning of a rescue organisation, where the decision-maker asked for the analysis to include an assessment of the benefit of the operations, so that alternative proposals could be judged. This meant placing a money value on the average human life. Now such figures do exist in some planning circles, morbid though it may seem to the reader who has not encountered them; but in this case the request was refused. The conclusions were stated in the form of 'so much cost to save so many lives', with no attempt to balance them. That is, the two criteria were kept separate. For it became clear that, whatever value the analyst put on a life and however well argued, each level of decision-maker was going to query it and replace it with his own value. This is the central difficulty: in spite of their brave words in giving him his terms of reference, the decision-makers are rarely prepared to delegate to the analyst the weight to put on each qualitative criterion.

So, in the Roskill case, there really was no alternative to publishing cost and noise nuisance values separately, each in their own units, for in a matter of this magnitude the decision will never be made on a single all-in cost comparison. The reasoned position came later from the Minister after the emotion had subsided:

We cannot put a precise monetary value on noise amelioration. The decision on what is reasonable will need to be taken on a broad judgement of the relation between the extent and degree of possible alleviation, and the price to be paid for them in terms of money, convenience, efficiency and time.

So here is the final decision-maker saying that he will take such decisions on four criteria at least. And I would argue that decisions can and will be made even if there is a much larger number of criteria all presented independently. This is the choice of method adopted by the Consumers' Association in their publication *Which?* Given the task of presenting multiple criteria comparisons on consumer goods, they simply set out all the value ratings of each criterion on a simple scale of from one to five 'blobs' – saying only that the more blobs the better – but always keeping them separate. They then give a short and heavily qualified assessment of 'the best buy' – more as an example to the reader of how to use the information for himself than as any global advice. No attempt is made to add up any of the blob ratings.

Adding up points awarded to each factor is a favoured approach to trying to get everything into one measure of goodness. I would fight almost to the death against this, but if it really has to be done, then the case for weighting (or rather the futility of not weighting at all) is shown in the following example.

Here the reader is invited to add up the ticks and conclude that, on points, soft contact lenses win. It seems astonishing that the same single point could be awarded for 'sensation of foreign body in the eye' and 'occasional oedema, staining, etc.' as for the enigmatic 'cheaper' and 'sterilisation simpler'. But if we try to give the separate factors a weighting, how

ADVANTAGES AND DISADVANTAGES OF HARD AND SOFT
CONTACT LENSES

Hard lenses	Advantage		Soft lenses
Hydrophobic		√	Hydrophilic
Hard surface for cornea – may give rise to sensation of foreign body in eye		√	Soft – little sensation in eye; no mechanical irritation
Impermeable to H_2O and O_2	√		Some degree of permeability
Cheaper	√		More expensive
Fitting quite straight-forward		√	Fitting simpler
Adaptation time necessary		√	No adaptation time
Acceptability good		√	Acceptability higher
Visual acuity good	√	√	Visual acuity claimed to be as good as with hard lens
Better for high degree of astigmatism	√		Use more limited by astigmatism
Limited wearing time		√	Longer wearing time
Corneal oedema, staining, etc. occasionally found due to over-wearing		√	Oedema claimed to be no problem
Resistant to mis-handling	√		More easily subject to damage
Sterilisation simple	√		Sterilisation still (till now) more complex
Storage between use simple	√		Must be stored in precisely isotonic saline

many points shall we give to this one, and how many to that one? Can we agree on the weights? Could we trust the analyst to set them himself *and not tell us?* I doubt it. And the reason we want him to tell us is because we shall want to change them to suit our own judgement, so nothing has in fact been gained. Independent criteria are independent, and combining them by whatever subterfuge will be little help to the decision-maker.

On the other hand, during the preliminary filtering stage of a study where there are a large number of alternative solutions to be evaluated, then all that I have said about the dangers of quantifying and combining different criteria may have to be disregarded. Reverting to the funnel diagram of Chapter 1, it is clear that the sharp narrowing-down on the left-hand side of the curves can often be done only by crude comparisons on a totally quantified basis. But when approaching the narrow point on the right, where the most likely solutions are beginning to emerge, and when the further filtering will be done in a dialogue with the decision-maker rather than by the analyst alone, then quantification and combination will tend to confuse rather than aid.

Apparently there are cases when a managerial team insists on taking a decision on the basis of a point-scoring system for the qualitative factors. Beattie and Reader mention this in the context of choosing a research and development programme, where they appear to have been successful in getting enough estimates on the different point scores, from a variety of managers, for the final decision team to be prepared to accept them as right. It may be that this is a special case. A similar philosophy is being adopted in a road-planning project in Norway, where the consensus of scores for different qualitative factors, gathered from the voting population, is being presented to the politicians along with the technical assessment. There is no report yet of whether this is assisting decision-making.

In a recent description of an advanced approach, B. C. Bishop suggests that the decision-maker should conduct a dialogue with a model, feeding it with weighted criteria so that it can search for a joint best solution, but readjusting the weightings as the shape of the solution emerges. This is a powerful idea, but I believe that it will be difficult for the decision-maker to know how best to adjust his weightings unless at each pass he is given not one but several alternative solutions to look at. Perhaps what is really being advocated here is a hope that the decision-maker can become more of an analyst so that he can be fully involved in the early filtering stage of the funnel diagram. This is clearly a good thing on the occasions when it is possible.

Let me close this chapter with the final delusion. More, perhaps, a delusion of the decision-maker than a self-delusion of the analyst, but none the less dangerous for that: 'It is bound to be better if it is put on to a computer.'

On the contrary, if there is a genuine choice between solving a problem manually or by computer, then it is almost certainly better done manually. Because then all the intermediate steps of calculation are checked and thought about as they are done; errors of logic or emphasis may be spotted even at a late stage in the numerical work; there is the opportunity to bend the calculations of particular cases to make them more realistic; there is the chance of avoiding the brittleness of inflexible methods. And above all, there is not the temptation to assume that just by putting in the input data and observing the output everything will be all right, and forgetting the imperfections of the program hidden inside the black box.

Fairly simple conceptual problems can get the best of both worlds by using a computer program to do the hard work of producing tables or sets of curves for each stage of the calculation, so that the user has the model set out in front of him on pieces of paper and can be as flexible as he likes in playing with the relationships involved. This can work well, for example in working out how best to carry out a fairly standard task according to constraints of time and cost. The modern but more expensive equivalent is an interactive computer program where the decision-maker himself sits at a terminal and has access to all the curves he wants. But here there is a further danger of hiding from view the calculations which are going on inside the machine, and deceiving oneself that as one sits at the console one is face to face with the truth.

Unhappily, there will be many occasions when there is no choice: the computer cannot be avoided, since the problem-solving work would be far too slow and laborious, if not impossible, without it. In this case we must bow to the inevitable, and when we have to then perhaps there is no real harm in permitting the decision-maker himself to swagger a little and say 'Look what my computer tells me', as if it were that much more likely to be true. As long as the analyst himself does not believe it.

7 The End Result

'... advice is a dangerous gift, even from the wise to
the wise, and all courses may run ill. But what would
you? You have not told me all concerning yourself; and
how then shall I choose better than you?'
              J. R. R. Tolkien, *The Lord of the Rings*

It is in the nature of things that the way in which
a study is concluded is closely bound up with the way
in which the conclusions are presented, and it is
convenient in this chapter to consider both how to
present results and how to keep to the deadline of
presenting them on time.

In earlier chapters I have urged the view that the
underlying objective of the study is to find a solution
which is not only correct but which can be implemented. It follows that, in presenting the conclusions
of the study, the underlying objective is to influence
opinion in such a way that the solution is seen to be
right and *will* be implemented.

Solutions which are right do not necessarily gain
acceptance on that count alone, even if they reach
the right audience – the ultimate decision-maker. If
the man presenting the conclusion is such an authority
on the subject, or possess so much self-confidence, or
merely has such a persuasive personality, it may be
that acceptance will flow naturally. It may be that a
written report is so clear and convincing that it
will gain acceptance without difficulty. But all this
flies in the face of experience; the average team
has to face the fact that acceptance is going to be
difficult, and that special skills of presentation will

be needed, not to say a tinge of guile and showman-
ship.

Finding out the nature of the audience is an essential first step, since what an audience will accept as
proof varies from one milieu to another. For example,
in studies of protectionism versus free trade in the
United States, it was complained that

> they are presenting their case in high-level papers,
> replete with graphs, econometric tables and alge-
> braic equations. These studies impress the experts
> but they make no impression at all in the places
> which really matter. . . .

It was pointed out that what 'the people that matter'
understand are the emotive phrases like 'sweated
labour' and 'export of jobs'. So the team should
report on a similar level – why should the devil have
all the best tunes? Again, hard facts may be clear
to a fully analytical mind, but the facts may have to
be supported with totally unscientific anecdotes
illustrating the point for another audience. The facts
by themselves may not be enough.

Going for a really hard sell is rarely excusable, since
by doing so the team are presuming an infallibility
of solution to the problem which rarely exists. If they
feel so passionately about their results as to start a
crusade, then the field is theirs, and anything goes –
as, for example, in the world environment debate
where it is clear that some teams are deliberately
exaggerating in the hope of triggering action. At a
lesser degree of intensity, and knowing the diluting
effect of transferring opinions from person to person,
plus the way in which ardour fades, it is not
unreasonable to find a persuasive spokesman or a
dynamic writer, and let him try to create enthusiasm.

When presenting forecasts, there is a particular

need to avoid an oversell, since the decision-maker may be unaware of the dangers of forecasting discussed in the previous chapter. The presentation must be scrupulous always to give the forecast in the conditional tense. For example, in a report of the Food and Agriculture Organisation of the United Nations, it is stated that 'If world agriculture production would rise by 2·5 per cent a year, the tendency for developing countries to provide a declining share of world exports would cease and might even be reversed.' Although this conditional gets rather laboured in a long statement, better that than switching back to 'will' or even 'should'. Use of 'would' makes even the lay reader realise that there are conditions attached which he ought to check before using the figure.

There is a wrong time to present the results of a study, finished or not. This may be when it is still too early for them to be acceptable. The presentation of results prematurely while the management uncertainties are still large can lead to a wasteful rejection of a sound analysis. This will be particularly true of in-house groups who have the possiblity of holding back their conclusions until there is a good hope that the decision-maker will be receptive to them.

It helps a great deal if a sizeable part of what one has to tell consists of truths which already have strong advocates within the decision-maker's organisation. Such allies are worth a lot, for they can keep the momentum going after the team has faded from view.

One of the most persistent and disappointing beliefs among both analysts and decision-makers is that the natural (and often only) culmination of a study is a written report. People in problem-solving groups are sometimes heard to remark (generally when putting forward a weak case for buying better office equipment): 'You see, our only output is paperwork.' This is empty-headed. The true output of the group is ideas. Paperwork is merely a traditional and highly inefficient vehicle for getting these ideas across.

This misbelief is fostered by the legal contract; when money changes hands there is felt to be the need for a tangible good which can be inspected and approved. Even when a contract is specifically for a service, 'To study the effect of X on Y', payment is often made on presentation of a piece of paper – as if it has to pass through a 'goods inwards' inspector. But if a report itself is found to be so bad that payment is refused, then the fault must surely be found in both parties to the contract. The dialogue described in Chapter 1 would have prevented such a situation arising. And this reintroduces one of the dominant principles of good reporting: if possible, take the decision-maker along gradually so that he is involved at all stages, including the report-drafting stage. He will then be thinking how to implement the conclusions before the report is written, and the report will merely serve as his reference material.

Teams perpetuate this reliance on the written report owing to conservatism and to convenience. Conservatism because everyone else does it (and shelves are full of dusty, yellowing reports to prove it). and convenience because the alternatives are more demanding. Of course, there is a great deal of value in a permanent record as a reference work, and in most cases this is precisely what it becomes. If this is the intention then the author can be content, but in the great majority of cases the report is written for much more dynamic reasons – to explain, to convince, and to encourage action. In this case the team should think twice before picking up their pens, because for those ends a report is a very poor instrument.

Sometimes a report is called for as a substitute for action; and at other times, particularly in some developing countries, the intention may have been genuine but there may not have been enough initiative to follow it up. Both these produce the same symptom: successive reports dealing with the same problem and often calling for roughly the same solution with no evidence that action has been taken as a result of the previous one. In the face of this symptom the group leader would be well advised either to avoid the problem, or else to opt for a more dynamic alternative than a report at the time the project is being designed.

If a report must be written, let it be in two volumes: one volume to be as dynamic, simple-minded and above all *short* as possible; the other as long and detailed as desired, since it will only be read by specialists and will certainly fill the role of reference material. Even this approach will rebound from time to time, as fellow analysts point out how naïve the first volume seemed to them, but this is by far a lesser evil then writing it in a way that the audience – the decision-maker – finds unintelligible or unmanageable. If there is a member of the team who is incurably 'an analyst's analyst', then let him stay with the second volume.

And indeed, there is the need for a good deal of over-compensation here against the tendency of a team to believe that what they have written is very simple when it is not. This is particularly true when the team has lived with the problem for some time and has forgotten what their state of mind was at the start. It has much in common with the frequent mistake of amateur composers of puzzles and treasure-hunts who try to set something easy but end up by making it fiendishly difficult, without realising it.

During editing, to search out flaws in the arguments being presented it can be useful to read the draft backwards, section by section. By proceeding from conclusion to supporting argument instead of in the more usual direction, the inconsistencies often show up more readily. It is also a way of injecting some freshness of thinking and logic which may be badly needed if the editor has been engaged in the project, since he has to supply his own rationale of the missing information at each reverse stage and is repeatedly brought up short and forced to re-think as he finds the written rationale is different. Reading backwards is not an entirely new idea, although it is normally done casually, rather than by design. Cherry quotes the story about Thomas Hobbes who became convinced of the truth of geometry by working backwards through Euclid's axioms. (The fact that several of Euclid's axioms are in fact fallacious weakens my point but does not destroy it, since it took a Bertrand Russell to point to the fallacies.)

In the simple but dynamic first volume the authors must fight to get their points across, but in doing this they must avoid allowing the decision-maker to go overboard on the conclusions. In a sense they should write so as to control his reaction, trying to avoid injecting a spurious certainty where there is none, and watching out for areas where conclusions can be taken wrongly. The usual cause of this is that the audience has failed to appreciate the assumptions on which the conclusions were based. So these must be spelt out. As I mentioned in an earlier chapter, it will be very much more valuable if the decision-maker has been introduced to the assumptions one by one as the study progressed, and does not have to stagger under the impact of all of them at once at the last moment.

There is also a trap in this two-volume approach into which I have myself fallen several times – each time for the same reasons, and in spite of having seen the danger coming. This is the tremendous temptation to produce a nearly final text of the first volume before drafting the second. Since the very act of writing down the technical detail of the second volume will most often trigger off a last round of research, the dynamic, pithy conclusions already enshrined in volume 1 are very likely to need re-slanting owing to this last stage of research. This can be time-wasting, and the alternative – of re-slanting volume 2 details to fit the conclusion – is out of order.

The reason why one falls into this trap in spite of knowing about it is undoubtedly the tendency to wishful thinking ('We already know the main conclusions. The rounding-off work for volume 2 won't affect them'). This is always plausible, but is too often proved wrong. Clearly, the solution is better discipline; this is one time when the methodological purist of Chapter 3 could perhaps be given a watch-dog role. There is something to be said for getting a full first draft of volume 1 and then holding it until all research is genuinely complete, but the introduction and summary sections will certainly have to be rewritten, and writing these too soon, however tempting, can be counter-productive.

What, then, are the alternatives to the much maligned written report? They come at once to mind if one considers that the project team want to *teach* the decision-maker something – to put forward the conclusions in such a way that he *learns* them, rather than merely receiving them passively and then forgetting.

Clearly, this demands the same methods as in any field of teaching. And as in teaching there is a wide choice. The main alternatives in face-to-face presentation are lessons, lectures and seminars.

The lesson, where the approach is informal and tries to set up a two-way flow between student and teacher, is normally the most effective in making sure that the student fully understands and remembers. It consists of interspersing instruction with questions which test comprehension and also with questions which teach by making the student reason a point out for himself. If the presentation could take this form it would be ideal, but since the 'students' will probably be senior management or, even more difficult, a mixture of several levels of management, it will normally be difficult to arrange.

The lecture is the least efficient in hammering home points since it is a one-way flow only, and even a brilliant lecturer with full visual aids is unlikely to leave the audience with more than half the information transferred. In higher education where lectures are most often used they constitute only one prong of the teaching process and are usually accompanied both by self-motivated private study and by tutorials.

The tutorial or seminar is a useful alternative. It reintroduces the two-way flow but leaves the student and teacher on almost level terms. Nor does it have to expose any individual manager who has not fully grasped a point. If the study conclusions could be organised in such a way that the seminar can be guided from stage to stage, with discussions and exercises which involve the management audience, bridging the gaps between stages so that the developing argument appears natural and accords with experience, then the project team have the maximum possible chance of seeing their solution implemented.

Whichever form of presentation is adopted (and usually it will be a hard fight to avoid anything but a lecture), enormous capital can be made from good visual aids. It is wise to earmark a proportion of project resources for the preparation of the presentation. There may be a tendency to ignore this in the budget and assume that it can be fitted in on group overheads, and that time will be found somehow. But just as report-writing figures in a project plan, so must any presentation activity which replaces or supplements the report.

The visual aids will normally only be projected slides of drawings and of simple texts which drive home a significant point, although the modern version of the old-fashioned epidiascope, which projects from source material, should not be overlooked. If there is the slightest opportunity to get hold of the services of a film team, then the improvement in the presentation will be dramatic. So often the analyst will want to demonstrate to the decision-maker a relationship which either changes with time or else is more than two-dimensional. For both of these a simple moving cartoon is ideal. There is no need to try to put the whole presentation on film. This is exorbitantly expensive and takes the personal touch away. For the maximum effect, a short cartoon of the vital relationship, plus projected slides, plus a blackboard, plus a model of some sort, should all be mixed in together. A standard is now being set in this type of presentation by television teaching, which will repay close examination.

When aids of any sort are used, it is fatal for them to go wrong or be poorly presented. The audience always judge by appearance, not by intentions, however unfair this is. (The cruellest case of this which I remember was when a brilliant engineer was demonstrating his advanced – and first in the field – bandwidth compression system for television transmission, and the first comment by a member of the audience was that the picture seemed very distorted, which was totally irrelevant to the demonstration and would only have meant adjusting the standard receiver controls.)

This need for a high standard of presentation can be irritating, since there is really not much more virtue in a slide properly drawn and annotated by a draughtsman than a hand sketch by the analyst himself. But in most cases the hand sketch will not be so well received; this seems to be a fact of life which has to be accepted.

Another form of aid is a specially designed nomogram or slide-rule. Quite a lot can be represented in this way, and teaching someone how to use it is one of the best ways of passing on an understanding of a relationship.

When the output of the project is a developed methodology to be handed over for use by someone else, an attempt should be made to programme the user through its application, otherwise all he has is a kit of tools (equations, tables, nomograms, computer programs) sitting in front of him and an almost unlimited way in which these tools can be used – some of which may be invalid. What is needed is a set of operating instructions for the methodological kit. A good write-up will always include one or two worked examples, but the danger is that a worked example may not state rigorously what the start and finish points are, what assumptions are being made at each stage, and what alternatives exist at each stage.

By a programmed methodology I mean something which may have a form such as:

Start: What is the aim of doing this? A, B or C?
           If A, then:
           1. Measure   ...
                          ...
                          ...
           2. Choose   ...
                          ...
           3. Set   ...
                          ...
                          ...
           4. Apply model X
           5. Find   ...
           6. Reset   ...
                          ...
           7. Apply model Y
              etc.
End: The conclusion is:
                          ...
                          ...
                          ...

It will help to give the project a sense of direction if at a quite early stage the need for, and the rough shape of, such a programme is thought about.

When, as a result of the project, the need arises to introduce a full new pattern of behaviour – a new information system, for example – then training will be needed rather than simply a presentation. This is a much wider issue which should be dealt with in a separate implementation project, and is outside the scope of the present work.

The issue of a report, or the holding of a presentation, will normally have been given a deadline, tied to the length of the project. The project start may have been rather blurred, but an effective date must have been agreed and so the end deadline will have been fixed. As this last milestone approaches, a decision will have to be made whether to keep to it or to abandon it.

Keeping to deadlines is a virtue and as a principle should be firmly laid down. But while it is good to have a reputation for always finishing projects on time, it is wrong to give this priority over getting the decision-maker to accept the results of the work. Clearly, if there is any reason to think that by continuing past the original end-date there is a higher probability of successful acceptance, then it would be pedantic to stop short with such precision (unless the resources have been so tightly planned that the team simply has to stop).

Indeed, the deadline is ofen a quite false one, picked almost out of the hat by the decision-maker at the start of the project, and signifies no more than: 'Don't go on for more than six months or you'll overspend.' In such cases going on a little longer without overspending is likely to be quite acceptable. I have found that when success is genuinely around the corner, a request for more time (for the same funds) is usually perfectly well received. There is a lifeprinciple here working for the team; all the world is incurably optimistic about schedules, and by the time the team's work is drawing to a close there is a strong chance that the event which the deadline was set to mesh with has itself slipped back by an equal amount. In fact a group could be forgiven for setting as an aim to be just a little better than the rest of the world in keeping to schedule, but not too much better; this could be their optimum policy, but I leave it to the reader to decide whether it is a worthy one.

When permission to overrun a deadline is given, there is an insidious tendency to ease up. Since this must result in the final overrun being even more than it would have been had the original deadline still been in force, there will now be a likelihood that the extended deadline will also be overrun. The cure for this – as in preventing the automatic consumption of contingencies – is the strong hint of failure in the air: partial failure on the first overrun; total failure on the second.

When on the other hand a deadline is overrun without permission, there is an even worse phenomenon – the over-the-hump effect. As the deadline recedes into the past it becomes even more remote than when it was in the future. It may cease to have any real effect on the progress of the work at all. It is as if the team says: 'Oh, well, in for a lamb, in for a sheep', and procedes at a more leisurely pace than ever to complete the work in the way that seems best. This is a phenomenon which *ought* to be impossible when funds are being consumed and project control is sound.

All this is far from the primary issue – keeping to deadlines. Overrunning deadlines is an emergency action, and the group leader should be much more concerned with keeping to them. This can be done in three ways: by discipline, by brinkmanship or by graceful degradation.

Discipline is achieved by a realistic method of project control. If methods such as I have described in Chapter 4 are applied, then it should not be too difficult to finish on time. The last milestone of all is a more important one than the rest and should be seen approaching with a keen concern from about half-way through the project. When the three-quarter mark is passed before the end-date is taken seriously, then the result is likely to be what I call brinkmanship.

Unhappily, brinkmanship is the more common method of keeping to a deadline the world over. It is characterised by always trying to squeeze in just a little more research, saying all the time 'It will all be ready on time, never fear', until it gradually dawns on the team that it will not. Then the project is extracted from its predicament by working round the clock like madmen. Some teams enjoy this end-of-project drama – although they will never admit it – since it gives a real wartime blitz spirit which is not all bad. And there may be environments in which it is a good idea. But not in problem-solving. Here it is rarely productive of the best work. During the last mad rush there is little time for careful thought, and just when a calm and rational judgement is most needed, to look at the conclusions as they are emerging, it is missing. Apart from broad judgements which can be damaged, there tend to be a number of minor errors as well.

A natural characteristic of this brinkmanship is to call in the big guns. The group leader and others start belatedly applying themselves to the project in detail, picking up the weaker and least finished parts of the work and rapidly strengthening them. But, as I mentioned when I discussed the pick-up approach as a method of ongoing project control, this is far less useful at the end, since however good the senior men are they cannot catch up months of falling behind in a few days, and they may have to take recourse in merely papering over cracks. This could conceal bad work deeply enough for it never to be found, but is not likely to produce good work.

Some increase in tempo during the last stage of a

project is normal and desirable. A build-up to a conclusion seems a natural human principle and there is no need to fight it. But it is wise to keep it within bounds. When brinkmanship is ruled out, but the deadline is still seen approaching too fast for comfort, the team is left with the third alternative – graceful degradation. The final project output is quite different from a product, where there is a physical specification to be met. There will be only a broad definition of what the scope of the answer is to be, and the precise level of detail will be a matter of judgement. There may be many less essential details which the team can cut out during the closing stages and so give themselves time to complete the main lines of work fully.

The existence of these fallback opportunities is easily understood by people working in the intellectual field, but is sometimes difficult to get through to others, even when it can be demonstrated that the fallback options were foreseen early in the project. The principle which has to be explained is that every problem could be examined at greater or lesser levels of detail, and that in setting up the project one particular level had been chosen out of this continuum. It was a reasonable level, but was a point of aim which did not have to be precisely reached for the project to be successful. It turned out to be just a little too ambitious, so the graceful degradation decision is to fall back to a slightly lower level, still meeting the requirement and still giving good value for money.

This argument is almost convincing, but a little thin. The truth of the matter is that it should never need to be deployed, since if regular and disciplined project control has been applied throughout, there will be no need for any special degradation during the terminal stages. There will be no sudden transition during the closing stage since the level of detail will have been continuously adjusted throughout the progress of the work.

References

page

7   *a peculiarly Russian trait*
    J. M. Bochenski, *Diamat* (Reidel, Holland, 1963).

13 *a rigid and hierarchical management style*
    D. McGregor, *The Human Side of Enterprise* (McGraw-Hill, 1960).

14 *Technology may so change the nature of man*
    H. Fruchtbaum, 'Technology: Tyrant or Liberator', *Journal of International Affairs*, xxv, no. 2, 1971.

20 *a row of 729 junior managers*
    A. Jay, *Management and Machiavelli* (Hodder & Stoughton, 1967 .

29 *everyone tends to rise to the level of his own incompetence*
    L. J. Peter and R. Hall, *The Peter Principle* (Morrow, 1969).

34 *two quite different character traits*
    A. Jay, op. cit.

55 *a project can be performed at a number of different rates*
    C. J. Beattie and R. D. Reader, *Quantitative Management in R & D* (Chapman & Hall, 1971).

56 *this form of natural structuring*
    A. Jay, *Corporation Man* (Jonathan Cape, 1972).

66 *a searching review of such methods*
    C. J. Beattie and R. J. Reader, op. cit.

69 *some meetings should be long and leisurely*

R. Townsend, *Up the Organisation* (Michael Joseph, 1970).

69   *every single utterance during a conversation*
C. Cherry, *On Human Communication* (Wiley, 1961).

78   *something of greater urgency than documentation*
Orientation Course in Mechanised Data processing (United Nations, New York, 1966: sales no. 66.II.H.3).

85   *Perhaps the best exponent of originality*
E. de Bono, (for example) *The Use of Lateral Thinking* (Jonathan Cape, 1967).

87   *part of the creative scene for many years*
E. Jantsch, *Technology Forecasting in Perspective* (O.E.C.D., Paris, 1967).

88   *techniques which generate a full list of alternatives*
F. Zwicky, *Morphology of Propulsive Power* (California Institute of Technology, 1962).

90   *a basic confusion which existed*
Documents of the Tenth Plenary Assembly, *C.C.I.R.*, IV, Report 211 (Geneva, 1963).

91   *an earlier attempt*
G. C. Tarr, 'Classification of the processes of modulation and transmission', *Transactions of the I.E.E.E.*, COM–12, 3, 108 (1964).

91   *entitled 'Artificial Imagination'*
A. Kaufmann, 'L'Imagination Artificielle', *Revue Française d'Informatique et de Recherche Operationelle*, vol. 3, p. 5 (1969).

92   *after drawing a morphological chart*
K. W. Norris, 'The Morphological Approach to Engineering Design', *Conference on Design Methods* (Pergamon, 1963).

94   *a recent seminar on innovation*
London Seminar of Professional Group E1
(Institution of Electrical Engineers, 1971).

99   *a striking example of a new conceptual framework*
O. I. Franksen, 'Mathematical Programming in Economics by Physical Analogues', *Simulation*, vol. 12, nos. 6 and 7.

100   *another example of conceptual thinking*
A. Ghosh and H. Sarkar, 'An input-output matrix as a spatial configuration', *Economics of Planning*, vol. 10, nos. 1–2 (1970).

101   *Jantsch's conclusion on brainstorming*
E. Jantsch, op. cit.

102   *The theory of human problem-solving*
A. Newell and H. A. Simon, *Human Problem-Solving* (Prentice-Hall, 1972).

103   *the point is discussed by McCall*
J. J. McCall, 'Probabilistic microeconomics', *Bell Journal of Economics and Management Science*, vol. 2, no. 2 (1971).

105   *This is unquantifiable*
H. Lever, quoted in the *Financial Times*, 12 July 1971.

109   *Pritsker and Kiviat classify models*
A. B. Pritsker and P. Kiviat, *Simulation with GASP II* (Prentice-Hall, 1969).

111   *the relevant scientific discipline of semiotics*
C. Cherry, op. cit.

112   *educated beyond realising*
I. Macbeath on the Industrial Relations Act, *The Times*, 15 Nov 1971.

113   *heuristic, intuitive and improvised*
J. Kornai, 'Man-Machine Planning', *Economics of Planning* (Norway), vol. 9, no. 3 (1969).

114 *The number of assumptions which could be made*
U. N. Economic Commission for Africa, *Working Group on Production Accounts Report*, E/C.N.14/46 (1971).

114 *The Predicament of Mankind*
D. H. Meadows *et al.*, *Limits to Growth* (Universe Books, New York, 1972).

122 *the so-called new art of futurology*
C. de Hoghton *et al.*, ... *and now the future* (a PEP Survey of Futures Studies, Aug 1971).

123 *a sad tale of sales forecasting*
J. M. Moroney, *Facts from Figures* (Penguin, 1951).

124 *research at this point even appears to have been concluded*
A. Menne, 'Some results of investigation of the syllogism and their philosophical consequences', *Logico-Philosophical Studies* (Reidel, Holland, 1962).

124 *prophets of doom are never shaken*
E. de Bono, op. cit.

126 *the existence of a correlation*
G. Bell, *The Times*, 21 June 1972.

129 *a very thorough attempt was made*
'The Cost of Noise', *METRA*, x, no. 1 (Mar 1971).

130 *the methodology would not tolerate infinite values*
M. E. Paul, 'Can aircraft noise be measured in money?', *Oxford Economic Papers*, vol. 23, no. 3 (Nov 1971).

132 Advantages and disadvantages of hard and soft contact lenses
The Optician, Apr 1972.

133 *a point scoring system for the qualitative factors*
Beattie and Reader, op. cit.

134 *the decision-maker should conduct a dialogue with a model*
B. C. Bishop, *O. R. Quarterly*, vol. 23, no. 3 (Sep 1972).

137 *they are presenting their case in high-level papers*
'The Washington Column', *The Times*, 21 Feb 1972.

138 *If world agricultural production would rise*
'Agricultural Commodities; FAO projections up to 1980', *Far East Trade and Development* (Nov/Dec 1971).

141 *the story about Thomas Hobbes*
J. Aubrey, *Brief Lives*, vol. 1 (1680), quoted in C. Cherry, op. cit.

141 *several of Euclid's axioms are in fact fallacious*
Bertrand Russell, *The Principles of Mathematics* (Allen & Unwin, 1903).

Subject Index

Accuracy:
  excessive pursuit of, 106
  of mechanistic description, 8
  of models, 112–13
  spurious, 97
Administrator:
  introduced, xii
  paperwork, 79
Analyst:
  introduced, xii
  the ideal, 32
  typical skills, 35
  working in isolation, 15
Applications men, 32
Arrogance, 32
Assumptions:
  and honesty, 113
  involving the decision-maker, 9
  plausible, 120
  recording, 77
  virtue of simplicity, 96

Bloodhound and terrier analogy, 34
Brainstorming, 67, 88, 94, 101
Brinkmanship, 148–50

Cellular structure, 1, 94
Changes of direction, 23, 84
Common sense, 105–6
Communication, 19, 48, 50–2, 80

Computer techniques, 95–6
  cf. manual methods, 134–5
  mystique, 106, 116–17, 135
Conceptual thinking, 98–101
Conclusions:
  presentation of, 136–7
  reconciling different viewpoints, 15
Confidence, 103
Contingencies, 81
Cost control, 80
Crash projects, 55–6
Creativity, 2, 85 ff.
  automatic, 91
Criteria:
  multiple, 128–33
  'rightness', 7
  unquantifiable, 129
  weighting, 131–4

Data:
  analysis, 42
  collection, 75
  lack of, 104
Deadlines, 146–8
Decision-maker:
  as a contributor, 9
  attitude towards forecasting, 124
  impressed by complexity, 98
  introduced, xi
  lack of authority, 12
  need for a dialogue, 3

Disagreements within a team, 15, 45, 70
Discussions, fruitful, 69
Disharmony, 37
Dogmatists, 45

Empiricism versus theory, 7
Evolution of a group, 25
Experts, 44

Failure, 109
Familiarisation, 74–5
Fanatics, 26
Filtering of solutions, 3, 128
Forecasting, 121–6
    trends, 123
    reluctance to believe in change, 124
Futurology, 122, 125

Group:
    evolution, 25, 49
    meetings, 51
    rate of growth, 29, 94
Group leader:
    and lagging activities, 72
    introduced, xi
    responsibilities, 22, 24
    role of, 18
    span of control, 30
Guesswork, 104–5

Hierarchies, 21
    in modelling, 119
Human motives, 6, 52–3

Implementation of solutions:
    influence of final report, 136
    lack of authority, 12
    poor solutions, 6

user's policy space, 12
uses of sophistication, 98
Information theory, 36
Intellectual cell, 15
Intellectual charity, 38, 40
Intellectual span, 18, 96
Intuition, 92

Junior staff, 42

Lateral thinking, 85–7, 101
'Limits to Growth' controversy, 114
Logical networks, 62, 66

Management style in problem-solving, 31
    Theory 'Y', 13
Meetings, 67–72
    group, 51
    progress, 67, 71
Milestones, 59, 65, 71–2, 75
Modelling controversy, 114
Models:
    accuracy, 117
    adapted for different purposes, 112
    calibration, 118
    classified, 109
    dialogue with, 134
    overemphasis, 115
    role of, 110, 113
    validation, 118
Modernisation of part of a system, 11
Morphological approach, 88–94, 101
Multi-disciplinary teams, 35

New staff, 50
Novel solutions, 2

Objectives, 45, 108
Optimisation, 127–8
Originality, 84
Overview, 41

Paperwork, 76–80
  administrative, 79
Parallel working, 56–8, 64–5, 97
Persistence, 102
Personal preferences, 25
PERT diagrams, 54, 60
Pick-up method, 72–3, 94
  at the end of a project, 151
Practical men, 49, 80
Pragmatic approach, 47
Presentations, 143–5
Problem boundaries, 81
Productivity in problem-solving, 56, 73
  and size of cell, 16
  definition, 54
Progress control, 72, 82–3, 148–51
Project co-ordinators, 40
Project leader:
  introduced, xi
  responsibility, 20–1
  role in co-ordinating thought, 16
Project plans, 59 ff., 113
Purity of approach, 46

Qualitative aspects, 1, 107

Random processes, 36
Recruiting, 26, 50
Report-writing:
  alternatives to written reports, 139, 142–5
  editing, 141
  layout, 140–2
  objectives, 136–8
  when to start, 60, 64
Reporting back, 47
Requirement definition, 4
Resistance to change, 11

Self-deception, 109
Seniority problems, 40, 42
Sensitivity tests, 114
Serendipity, 58, 63, 87
Simplicity, 96–7
  in report-writing, 140
Social aspects of a problem, 6, 41
Social responsibility, 13
Socal sciences, 36
Specialists contributing to a project, 21
Staleness, 25
Stallion and mare analogy, 34
Standard techniques, 84, 112
Statistical correlation, 126
Symbolic models, 111
System description:
  level of sophistication, 112
  the 'Aunt Sally', 76
  validity of models, 111
Systems men, 34

Team size, 16
Technical notes, 78–9
Techniques:
  dangers, 95
  devotees, 34
  over-sophistication, 112
  untried, 58
Technology, danger of, 14
Tempo of working, 54–7, 63
  in the closing stages, 149–150

Think-tank approach, 1
Time-sharing between projects, 63

Traditional beliefs, 10
Tribal instincts, 39

Vertical thinking, 85, 101